POPULAR CULTURE IN AMERICA

1800-1925

POPULAR CULTURE IN AMERICA

1800-1925

Advisory Editor
DAVID MANNING WHITE

Editorial Board
RAY B. BROWNE
MARSHALL W. FISHWICK
RUSSEL B. NYE

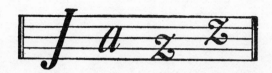

by P A U L   W H I T E M A N
and
MARY MARGARET M^cBRIDE

ARNO PRESS
A New York Times Company
New York • 1974

Reprint Edition 1974 by Arno Press Inc.

Reprinted from a copy in the University
of Illinois Library

POPULAR CULTURE IN AMERICA: 1800-1925
ISBN for complete set: 0-405-06360-1
See last pages of this volume for titles.

Manufactured in the United States of America

———◆———

Library of Congress Cataloging in Publication Data

Whiteman, Paul, 1890-1967.
    Jazz.

    (Popular culture in America)
    Reprint of the 1926 ed. published by J. H. Sears,
New York.
    1. Jazz music.   I. McBride, Mary Margaret,
joint author.   II.   Title.   III.   Series.
ML3561.J3W46 1974   785.4'2'0973   74-15753
ISBN 0-405-06387-3

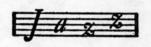

THE JAZZ DYNASTY

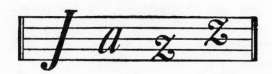

by PAUL WHITEMAN

and

MARY MARGARET McBRIDE

Illustrated

J. H. SEARS & COMPANY, INC. 1926

NEW YORK

CONTENTS

CONTENTS

LIST OF ILLUSTRATIONS

LIST OF ILLUSTRATIONS

I
Beginnings

I: Beginnings

*J*AZZ came to America three hundred years ago in chains. The psalm-singing Dutch traders, sailing in a man-of-war across the ocean in 1619, described their cargo as "fourteen black African slaves for sale in his Majesty's colonies." But priceless freight destined three centuries later to set a whole nation dancing went unnoted and unbilled by the stolid, revenue-hungry Dutchmen.

For that matter, the negroes themselves knew no more of jazz than their masters. In their tropical home, up to the day a hostile tribe fell upon them, they had been accustomed to make a joyful noise with voice and drums to gods who supplied corn and game plentifully. They had performed their labors to the throb of the tom-tom and measured off their journeys to the rhythm of a zither.

Suddenly the gods had become angry, delivering their bewildered worshipers to an enemy. The

3

blacks, harnessed each to his neighbor by a clanking weight, were too frightened to remember the songs of propitiation their fathers had sung, and besides, their drums had been broken in war. They understood, indeed, scarcely anything of their plight except that they had been traded to the Dutchmen for beads and rum by men as black as themselves.

They had never heard of the great "New World" for which Spain and France and England were fighting. They knew only that it was very cold on the ocean after the warmth of their own hot, sunny plains.

Even Virginia, brightest and gayest of the colonies and the first to buy negro slaves, seemed dreary and bleak to the Africans. So song fled from their lips—yet only for the time. Jazz, although they did not know it, was part of their heritage and was to be their gift to an alien posterity.

The thrifty Dutch traders, after they had successfully disposed of their human wares and unwittingly assured a future for jazz, returned home to put their money in the bank and to repair piously to church and praise the Lord for his goodness.

Beginnings

Meantime to the virgin continent in 1619 were hurrying the strongest and most courageous spirits of Europe—and the failures, criminals and good-for-nothings. The best of those who came were ambitious, restless adventurers escaping from the traditions and restrictions of the Old World. They brought little of elegance or culture to their new home; they were interested in something they regarded as more vital. They wanted a different order and they wanted it quickly. There was chaos and change in Europe then, following the great wars, just as there is to-day; but the settlers of America wanted more change and they were not willing to wait for it.

There was great need for youth and spirit in the New World. Food, clothing, shelter—the whole of existence—had to be wrested from the soil. Easy short cuts to living were out of the question. The man who would not work literally would not be able to eat.

And so those who had come to realize ideals and those who had come to forget them joined from necessity in the sharp struggle for the essentials of life. Temporarily, at least, the New

World was a completely materialistic proposition. Even if there had been a desire for it, there was no leisure for elegance where mere living was so precarious. True, the immigrants who poured in later brought whatever of culture they had; but these thin streams were soon lost in the immense tide of crude hard work. Aristocracy was of strength and youth, not of breeding, wealth or art.

Under the stimulus of the vast resources and thrilling struggles with Indians and wilderness, the disillusioned gradually grew hopeful and the hopeful buoyant. It seemed there was nothing the rich land could not be made to produce. When the pioneers had done what they could with their hands, they at length turned to making machinery, impatient to enjoy better and more luxurious living.

Expansion, invention, booms became the fashion of the times. People began to enjoy more comforts in America than anywhere else in the world. The mind of the country grew more and more ingenious. We became and have remained the most inventive nation. A diligent statistician recently revealed that in a single year when 5,807 patents were issued in this country, Germany, next on the list, had only 1,083. Another demon tabulator has estimated that without American inventions it would take the hands of one billion persons or two-thirds of the population of the world working ten hours a day to manufacture all the merchandise consumed by the peoples of the earth, whereas now it takes only fifty million persons!

The busy, growing days brought forth daily wonders. Fulton's steamboat was throwing open the Hudson and finally making ocean travel a more speedy and comfortable proposition. The locomotive, fearfully called a devil's invention because it ran at the unheard-of speed of fifteen miles an hour, developed from an awesome miracle to a commonplace necessity. Lightning had come down Ben Franklin's kite string, and was soon electrifying the continent. The rhythm of machinery became the rhythm of American civilization— a clanging, banging, terrific rhythm, full of an energy that promised accomplishment. Even the climate, with its sudden changes from hot to cold, its cyclones and thunderstorms, proved more invigorating than the climate anywhere else.

Soon there was food and to spare for everybody.

Machines developed a material civilization with unheard-of rapidity. Through them, too, was built up a leisure class and the beginnings of an aristocracy of wealth. A demand for luxuries followed and the machines supplied them. The machines supplied everything but beauty—the beauty of art, music, literature.

So far, there were no American arts. The pot into which had been tossed many fragments of culture had never been heated to the blending point. Such poetry, sculpture and music as grew up in the new land originated unmistakably in Europe. Yet the young country held rich material. The great melting pot was every day receiving the substance of a nation finding itself.

The brew needed no longer to rely, for richness, upon foreign-grown ingredients. And the leisure class was demanding ways to spend its money—beautiful homes, books, paintings. It imported British novelists, Italian architects, French dressmakers.

So little heed was paid to the premonitory bubblings of the melting pot that stunned amazement greeted its boiling over with the poetry of

Whitman, blunt, unconventional, startling; the short story of Hawthorne and Poe, compressed, vigorous, dramatically telling; the skyscraper, pile upon pile of steel and stone reaching toward the heavens, dwarfing all the puny efforts of the past, crude as the New World itself, yet satisfying in its power, its magnificent energy.

If there was surprise over these outpourings, there was positive horror over the next, which was *jazz*. Jazz, given its start in life by the righteous old Dutch traders, had been biding its time among the black laborers in the cotton fields of the lordly Southern planters and the negroes lounging in the sunshine along the New Orleans levees. It had lost none of its primitive African swing through mingling with the clanging of the machinery, the broken crashing rhythm of Whitman's poetry, the gigantic steel and stone of the skyscrapers. It was at once barbarous and sophisticated—the wilderness tamed to the ballroom.

A hundred million people seized it and began to sing and dance to it. Ministers, educators, organizations pitched into it vigorously—called it barbaric, demoralizing, degrading. A thousand headlines daily proclaimed that it was dying—was dead—and ten thousand saxophones promptly mocked the premature rumor.

Americans were ashamed of the upstart. They kept humming it absent-mindedly, then flushing and apologizing. Nothing so common could be esthetic, insisted the highbrows. Like everything else that was our own, its merits were, we thought, questionable. So it was left to Europe to discover the possibilities of our creature.

After Darius Milhaud had worked jazz motifs into his "La Creation du Monde" and Igor Stravinsky had written a jazz piece called "Ragtime," American musicians began to look interested. Perhaps, mused they, there is more to this strange invention than we have thought. But what is this jazz thing? Where did it come from? Where is it going?

The questions are still being asked, though jazz has been more or less taken into the bosom of society. They have been put to me so often that in self-defense I have set about trying to find some kind of answer that will be adequate. That's all this book is meant to be—an answer to the ques-

Beginnings

tions people have asked me about jazz and my connection with it. I have not attempted to put on style—I certainly haven't tried to be literary for I am no writer, but only the conductor of a jazz orchestra.

I sincerely believe in jazz. I think it expresses the spirit of America and I feel sure it has a future —more of future than of past or present. I want to help that future pan out. Other Americans ought to be willing to give jazz a respectful hearing. If this effort of mine helps toward that end, I shall be satisfied.

II

The Mango Seed

II: The Mango Seed

A BROWN-SKINNED Indian fakir stands in the midst of a half-bored, half-curious street crowd. In his hand is a mango seed. His face inscrutable, his heavy-lidded mysterious eyes narrowed to slits, he makes a few motions and before the eyes of those who watch, the mango seed sprouts, grows, buds, blossoms and bears fruit, all in the space of a scant sixty seconds.

America has a magic mango in jazz. One moment jazz was unknown, obscure—a low noise in a low dive. The next it had become a serious pastime of a hundred million people, the favorite diversion of princes and millionaires. Only just as it took centuries to produce the mango seed, so has it taken all of human life to bring forth jazz. The most primitive and the most modern combine in it. For hundreds of years, savage tribes in far places rolled out rhythms on harsh drums of home-

15

tanned hides, rhythms that stimulated to war or soothed to peace as the need of the moment dictated. The vitality of the world's youngest nation has absorbed, added to, and carried on that rhythm, first in ragtime and blues, now in jazz.

There was every reason why jazz should have burst upon a startled world at the touch of a hundred or more orchestra leaders in 1915. The time was ripe for almost any explosion. The war spirit was on the loose. The whole tempo of the country was speeded up. Wheels turned like mad. Every factory was manned by day and night shifts. Americans—and the term included Slavs, Teutons, Latins, Orientals, welded into one great mass as if by the gigantic machines they tended—lived harder, faster than ever before. They could not go on without some new outlet. Work was not enough and America had not yet found out how to play. The hard-pressed, hard-working young country had no folk songs, no village dances on the green. The incredible pressure was bound to blow off the lid and it might conceivably plunge a whole nation into nervous prostration or insanity. Psychologists, real and pseudo, sensing this danger,

16

issued long technical warnings, quoting their master, William James, on the peril to mental machinery of stimuli which, upon being received and recorded, are not acted upon.

Meanwhile was brewing in New Orleans a restorative for the national nerve complaint. The great American noise, jazz, was then just drifting out of the shanties and tango belt to begin its ascent into the ballrooms of the cultured. A showman, Joseph K. Gorham, gets credit for first realizing the possibilities of the underworld waif.

Gorham, a newcomer to New Orleans, heard a group of musicians playing on the street to advertise a prize fight. He was halted first by the perspiring, grotesque energy of the four players. They shook, they pranced, they twisted their lean legs and arms, they swayed like mad men to a fantastic measure wrung from a trombone, clarinet, cornet and drum. They tore off their collars, coats and hats to free themselves for a very frenzy of syncopation. As a finger-snapping black listener put it, they played "like all the debbils was atter 'em."

With the sure instinct of the good showman,

Gorham pushed his way through the crowd and interviewed the leader. He discovered that not one of the players in Brown's orchestra, as the odd group called itself, could read a note of music. Nevertheless, the showman knew that he had made a find and he listed the conductor's name with an address on Camp Street for future reference. He did not then note down the aggregation as a jazz band, though he undoubtedly knew the word as a slang phrase of the underworld with a meaning unmentionable in polite society. Probably it had never then been applied to a band. The rise of the term was interesting. It reached the drawing room finally on the strength of its terse expressive virility. On the way up, it was variously a verb and a noun, generally denoting speed or quick action of some kind. It appears now to be firmly established as a member of that long list of American words in good social standing that began their careers in the depths of moral and social disgrace.

Brown's orchestra was never officially labeled jazz, I believe. There is considerable discussion over exactly who did invent the term, "jazz band," with many authorities giving the honor to Bert

Kelly of Chicago, who described a group of musicians that he hired out to the Boosters' Club at the Hotel Morrison in Chicago as a "jazz band." The Boosters' Club promptly raised all its prices, alleging that the new-fangled jazz came high.

But before this, Brown's orchestra had been taken over by Mr. Gorham and placed at Lamb's Café, also in Chicago. The players burst upon the unsuspecting pork-packer world with a bang that nearly shattered the roof. The manager discreetly telegraphed Mr. Gorham to call off his band. Gorham, worried, rushed to send two wires, one to the manager counseling patience, the other to his band, telling them to ease down a little.

Apparently they did, for they were allowed to stay on with great profit to themselves and the establishment, people being turned away in droves. This, so far as I can discover from cabaret history, was the honest-to-goodness beginning of jazz.

Since Mr. Kelly's experiment with the word, there have been hundreds of attempts to find a new name for modern American music, but the public refuses them all. They are used to "jazz" and the word expresses something the music seems to mean.

J a z z

I cannot see that it matters much. Sometimes I have regretted the origin of the word because I think it probably has stirred up sentiment against the music. But if jazz turns out to be a good product, it won't really make much difference what it is called. Words, like men, slip down or climb up in the world and when a word has made good and stands for something real and worth while, I would never be the one to bring up its past against it.

It is a relief to be able to prove at last that I did not invent jazz. I took it where I found it and I wish the preachers and club lady uplifters who put on sheets and pillow cases to go jazz-klanning wouldn't concentrate on me. I don't deserve it, really, nor the snorting editorials from Burma to Sydney, either.

All I did was to orchestrate jazz. If I had not done it, somebody else would have. The time was ripe for that. Conditions produce the men, not men the conditions. It merely happened that I was the fortunate person who combined the idea, the place and the time. At least, I think I was fortunate. Others are not so sanguine.

The Mango Seed

The details of my family and home life are perhaps not important to anybody except myself, but I shall relate some of them here partly because, like everybody else, I enjoy recalling my youth, and mostly because of the stories I am always having to deny about my early life. Apparently jazz gives you a past whether you've had one or not. I should at least like folks to know that Mother and Dad did their best for me and that their best was very fine, even though I did take to jazz.

Wilberforce J. Whiteman, my father, is the best-balanced man I know. For thirty years, he was director of musical education in the Denver schools. He never had a drink until he was fifty-five and never smoked until he was sixty. Yet he wasn't priggish in the least. He has always been keen on athletics and was really proud of me the time the Denver Y. M. C. A. named me among a dozen physically perfect fellows in the gym class. He was plumb disgusted when I began to get fat and used to try to make me box it off.

Mother sang in oratorio and in the Denver choirs when I was growing up, managing a home and a career easily before women began to make so much of the idea. Her singing was always an enchantment to me. She used to rehearse while she cooked and she certainly could—and can—cook. Her mince pie would hold any home together, and as for her pop-overs—well, in my time I have gone from New York to Denver for a pop-over.

My mother is more than six feet tall and comes of a family noted for height. Her father, Sam Dallison, was a yeoman in Queen Victoria's guard. He was six feet three inches tall, and his five sons, born in this country, were all over six feet. My father's name was originally Wightman and on that side of the house, I am a mixture of Irish, Scotch, English and Holland Dutch.

I was, then, actually born into music, though I can't say I take much stock in the family stories that no matter how mad I was as a kid, I would always stop squalling to listen to a soprano voice. And I expect the doting aunt who claims that I used to cry to the chromatic scale is gifted with a loyal imagination. As for the legend that I jiggled my feet to "Hearts and Flowers" at the age of six months—well, that's on a par with the picture of me at the same period sitting naked in a bowl.

22

Both the legend and the picture, to my great embarrassment, used to be trotted out for company until I got old enough to make an effective stand against such indignity.

Better admit that I was no prodigy, even if I did love music from the first time I heard it. Perhaps I got the taste when I accidentally rolled down a Colorado mountain with a violin and a watermelon at the age of nine months. But more likely I inherited the music part, at least.

An astrologist friend looked at the stars on my birthnight (March 28, 1890) and predicted that I would have a stormy career. I've often wondered if she meant jazz. She said the planets were all whizzing cater-cornered when I was born. There were also a number of hurricanes, cyclones and earthquakes in places like Portugal, Gautemala and Buffalo. Nellie Bly went round the world in seventy-two days that year and a branch of the Woman's Christian Temperance Union was founded in Cleveland.

I have one sister, Ferne, who started taking vocal lessons when I got my first violin. Luckily we lived in a big house with wide lawns between us and the neighbors. Cooped up in a New York apartment house, I shudder to think where we'd have landed. In a police court probably. Even as it was, a new neighbor once rushed over pell-mell in answer to what he mistook for a frantic call for help. Sis and I were practicing a high note simultaneously.

The house was always full of brass bands and singers touching high C, partly family and partly guests. I began making my share of the family noises when I was three. On my toy violin, Dad taught me to pick out some tunes that I used to play for company. I had to wear velvet pants and submit to being patted on the head by dear old ladies; but I was a roughneck just the same and fairly accurate with my fists, so the fellows knew better than to call me sissy. I guess they wouldn't have anyway, though, come to think of it, for most of them liked music nearly as well as I did.

That was Dad's doing. Before he got through explaining music to them, every kid in Denver was crazy for a trombone or a French horn. He told the taxpayers they ought to finance music in the schools, just as they did plumbing, and finally they began to. A rich man named Wilcox got so interested in the idea that he put up the money to buy instruments and instruction for boys who couldn't afford them and we had some corking amateur orchestras. Father organized oratorio orchestras, too, and we all played in those. I was in one from the time I was ten.

Lots of boys who got their musical training from Dad make good money jazzing now. I've had some of them in my orchestra. I often think how lucky I was to grow up in Denver. In most places, I'm quite sure the boys of my generation would have tabooed oratorio orchestras as sissy and I wouldn't have wanted to disagree with the crowd. That would have been a tragedy, not because the world would have lost anything in losing me as a musician, but because I would have lost the thrill of doing the thing I do best and like most. There is nothing so sad to me as a misfit—a man or woman who hates his or her job and mopes at it.

Naturally as a youngster, I had no aspiration toward missionarying and the idea of some day trying to convert America to music as a he-man's interest wouldn't particularly have appealed to me as an ambition, even had I thought of it.

Yet that's what jazz is doing to-day and I am glad to feel that whatever I contribute is helping the good work along. It was just a question of time, though, until somebody would have attempted to put jazz on a real musical footing. If I had not, then some other boy from Denver might have. Or if not from Denver, then from one of the other rare spots in America where honest-to-gosh boys took music as part of their lives, real as the ole swimmin' hole or stealing watermelons.

My notion is that the chief contribution of the white American to jazz so far has been his recognition of it as legitimate music. And he would never have seen beauty in it if he had always set music up on a pedestal as something too high and holy for everyday life. The trouble with people who think of music in that way is that they don't really know its history or its meaning in terms of human life. They are ignorant worshipers of European culture or imitators of it. They complain that Americans have no art because we are not content to borrow or steal the admirable and beautiful things of another land.

Our attitude does not necessarily mean that we

do not appreciate what other countries have done, but why shouldn't we scout around a bit for ourselves, pioneer fashion? I didn't get the pioneering instinct very early, of course. Like all kids, I hated to practice and at seven, when I was graduated to a better instrument, I was supposed to practice an hour a day. Seemed as if I always had something important on hand when that hour came round and pretty soon I was deliberately cutting. The report of my defection, as those things will, seeped through to the head of the house. He called me on the carpet. I explained, with what I thought was logic, that I didn't like to practice.

He fixed me with a cold eye. I fidgeted, expecting chastisement then and there. But he only said: "Well, Mother, we can lead the horse to water, anyway." From then on, every afternoon, I was locked into Mother's sewing room with my fiddle. I sulked and threatened to run away to sea. Nobody made any objection. In fact, nobody paid a great deal of attention to me, except to see that I was locked up promptly.

Then I had another inspiration which I quickly put into action. I smashed the violin, banging its head over the flywheel of the sewing machine. The explosion was most satisfactory, something like a custard pie factory blowing up. The family noticed me all right that time. And Dad invited me to the woodshed.

Later he said: "Son, you can put in your practice hour to-morrow cutting the lawn. You know you've got to pay me back what that violin cost." At the end of five years, I was still sawing wood to pay for that expensive instrument!

As I got older, music affected me kind of like a fever. I couldn't even bear to hear Mother sing the "Erlking" around the house. If I were taken to the opera, I was sick and weak for a whole day afterward. Perspiration stood out all over me as soon as the music began and I was like a person in a trance until it stopped.

It is a good deal like that even to-day. "Parsifal" is my favorite opera, but I'm little good for a week after hearing it. I have always thought it would be a pleasant way to end this existence if one died listening to that immortal music. Yet these days I mostly go to a musical comedy, or a laugh show, if I have a night off. They are safety valves. That is why they are so well patronized. So is jazz a safety valve.

As a boy, my heroes were Paderewski, Harold Bauer, Kreisler and Isaye. I was taken to hear them when they played in Denver and sometimes was allowed to go with my father back stage. They were always simple and cordial. Kreisler once let me play his violin and indulgently asked if I liked its tone. The others were just as kindly and unaffected. That seems to be the way of the truly great. I have yet to see a real genius with the big head.

I must here confess for the first time to a thwarted ambition. Once I had all my plans set to become a mechanical engineer. In my spare time I tinkered with engines, but not very successfully. For instance, I made a motorcycle and forgot to put on the pedals and brakes. And I built a launch that would run everywhere except in water. My summers were spent in such experiments at a farm we had up in the mountains. I lived outdoors and hunted, fished and swam. I guess it is a good thing I inherited a certain musical knack from my parents, for I lack stick-to-itiveness. Yet I invariably admire most the hard things. That is what first attracted me to jazz. The popular idea is that jazz is a snap to play. That is all wrong. After you have mastered your instrument, it is easy enough to qualify in a symphony by following the score as written. But a jazz score can never be played as it is written. The musician has to know how to give the jazz effect.

The nearest to jazz I can remember as a boy was a thing called "Tale of a Bumblebee," which made an impression on me because the title page was decorated with a bumblebee sharpening his tail on a grindstone.

At sixteen I started ragging—of course we hadn't heard of jazzing then—the classics. A friend and I won a good deal of notice with this trick from the older members of the Denver symphony in which I had then begun to play. They used to keep us at it for hours. Our favorite classic for jazzing was the "Poet and Peasant" overture.

The warden of the Nebraska Insane Asylum heard us and thought our music might soothe his patients. He invited us down for a week-end at the asylum and we played all the pieces we knew.

We made a great hit, especially with an old fellow who called himself Nero. He had a fiddle of his own and tried to imitate us. I have heard jazz opponents say that Nero probably jazzed while Rome burned. I'm sure this Nero would have, if there had been any Rome to burn.

I got my education in music from my father and the teachers he selected. All were serious and talented musicians. One was Max Bendix, for whom I worked later in the San Francisco symphony. I can't remember the time when I didn't know the feel of a bow in my hand, and my first lesson was taken from my father when I was such a baby that I actually have no recollection of it.

At seventeen I was chief viola player in the Denver symphony, and three years later I went to the Pacific Coast to seek adventure. I found the excitement I craved in the San Francisco exposition and played with the World's Fair orchestra until the exposition closed. I was at the same time a member of the Minetti String quartette. When the exposition ended, I looked around for something new to do. By that time I was dissatisfied with symphony work. The pay was poor and there was little chance for initiative. And then—along came jazz!

We first met—jazz and I—at a dance dive on the Barbary Coast. It screeched and bellowed at me from a trick platform in the middle of a smoke-hazed, beer-fumed room. And it hit me hard. I had been blue all day, starting with the morning when I got out of bed on the wrong side. I am superstitious sometimes and that was one of the times. I cracked my shaving mirror. There was a button off my coat. My coffee was cold, my three-minute egg hard-boiled. I spilled the salt. It rained. At rehearsal my fiddle went blooey. A wisdom tooth jumped. When the old second violinist groaned that a musician's life is a dog's life, I bitterly agreed.

By evening I wanted nothing but bed or the Bay. Then Walter Bell, a fellow musician, dropped in and said, "Let's make a night of it."

"You may make a whole week of it if you like," I grouched. "I'm going to bed."

But Walter was a determined man and he was set on taking me out with him. Brute force finally won. Walter picked the jazziest of the jazz places—to cheer me up, he said. We ambled at length into a mad house. Men and women were whirling and twirling feverishly there. Sometimes they snapped their fingers and yelled loud enough to drown the music—if music it was.

My whole body began to sit up and take notice. It was like coming out of blackness into bright light. My blues faded when treated to the Georgia blues that some trombonist was wailing about. My head was dizzy, but my feet seemed to understand that tune. They began to pat wildly. I wanted to whoop. I wanted to dance. I wanted to sing. I did them all. Raucous? Yes. Crude—undoubtedly. Unmusical—sure as you live. But rhythmic, catching as the small-pox and spirit-lifting. That was jazz then. I liked it, though it puzzled me. Even then it seemed to me to have vitality, sincerity and truth in it. In spite of its uncouthness, it was trying to say something peculiarly American, just as an uneducated man struggles ungrammatically to express a true and original idea.

I wanted to know jazz better and it was immediately clear that I was going to. Coming, as I did, from an environment where music was taken for granted as a sort of daily necessity, jazz never did really shock me. It only worried and obsessed me. The fantastic beat drummed in my ears long after the strident echoes had died, and sleep for nights became a saxophonic mockery. Strains pestered me like a hunch you can't get the hang of.

In those first days I never thought seriously of taking up jazz playing, yet in the back of my mind was the conviction that I ought to turn over a new leaf soon if I wanted to amount to anything. It was one of those crises that, I suppose, come into every boy's life. You get to a place where you wear out your interest in all the things you are used to doing and need something fresh and exciting to keep you from becoming a loafer and a ne'er-do-well. At least it was so with me.

If I stayed with the symphony, I was pretty sure to continue following the line of no resistance. A viola player could go little further than I had already gone. Ready-made scores and methods of playing made it unnecessary for me to attempt any originality. And I had such stores of vitality to be turned into some channel. If there was no chance for it to go into my work, it was likely to

be diverted to wild parties. It was a requisite of
a good symphony player in those days that he be
a good drinker, anyway—and that he be a good
buyer of drink for his superiors.

Don't imagine for a moment that all this mor-
alizing was clearly worked out in my mind. I only
knew that I was listless, dissatisfied, despondent.
Of course I had money troubles, too. All of us
had. We often took extra jobs to make ends meet.
I drove a taxicab myself for a while, and even
then was usually broke.

Then jazz stepped in.

I have to smile when I start presenting jazz in
the rôle of reformer. I hope no reader will hiss
us off the page. I have often felt, when peda-
gogues and parents were panning my protégé, that
I ought to speak up and defend it as a moral agent.
Because it did pick me up and, more or less, in the
good old phrase, "make a man of me."

Not that I cherished any such hopes of it. I
began to experiment with the new music because it
was interesting. That is to say, soon after I heard
jazz for the first time, I resigned my job with the

symphony and applied at Tait's in San Francisco
for a place in a jazz band.

I got it and for two days lived in a sort of daze.
The thing that rattled round me like hail wasn't
music in the sense I had known it. I couldn't understand it—couldn't really get the hang of it.
But others were getting it—fat-faced men who
had never in their lives listened to any music except cheap thin popular tunes—rouged, young-old
women who had never once heard a real concert.
Something happened to them, just as it had happened to me that first night—something that shook
off their false faces and made them real and human,
spontaneous and alive for once. It wasn't altogether sex appeal, either. What on earth was it?

"Jazz it up, jazz it up," the conductor would
snort impatiently at about this point in my reflections. And I would try, but I couldn't. It was as
if something held me too tight inside. I wanted to
give myself up to the rhythm like the other players.
I wanted to sway and pat and enjoy myself just as
they seemed to be doing. But it was no good.

The second day the director fired me. He was
kind enough, but brief.

"You can't jazz, that's all," he told me. I nodded dully, watching the red hat of a girl at the other end of the room bobbing in an ecstasy of syncopation. Then I walked out of Tait's mild as milk and went home to my hall bedroom and slept. I slept clear around the clock. When I woke up, I was mad.

So they said I couldn't jazz, did they? Well, I'd show 'em. I'd learn to jazz. I'd learn if it took a year.

You know the thirst for knowledge that attacks the ambitious young man in the advertisement, when he reads about mail-order training courses? I felt just like that; but though there are plenty of them now, there were no correspondence-school jazz courses then, so I had to invent a method of educating myself.

This was to visit the restaurants where jazz was being played. A difficulty arose here. I had no money and they expected you to order food and drink in all those places. My old awe for head waiters increased during this time about a thousand-fold. They were so muscular. I had never noticed what brawny fellows a restaurant uses for headwaitering. In an argument with them, one would be nowhere at all.

Luckily I had a fairly presentable dress suit left over from symphony days. In this, I made a moderately prosperous-looking figure and there really was no way that a head waiter who didn't know me could tell that I hadn't a dime in my broadcloth pocket.

My cue was to appear when the music was at its height. I would hang around the entrance as though waiting for somebody, but really studying the orchestra. If necessary, I would make an effort to get a special kind of table such as head waiters give only to best-paying patrons. Of course, without the proffer of kale, I had no chance, and thus my way would be paved for an indignant retreat. The drawback was that this trick couldn't be used more than once on a restaurant.

These, as you might say, mere snatches of study, I eked out with experiments in my hall bedroom. Two landladies put me out during this period, on complaint of tenants above and below; for I experimented with my violin, as well as with paper and pencil. There were no saxophone-proof apart-

THE KING OF JAZZ DONS HIS CHAPS

ments in those days. No wonder the architect who invented them stands to make a fortune.

After many attempts, I finally worked out an orchestration and learned what I wanted to know about faking. Faking was what the early jazz orchestras relied upon. That is, they had no scores, each man working out his part for himself, "faking" as he went along. Up to that time, there had never been a jazz orchestration. I made the first and started into the jazz orchestra business. That sounds simple, but it wasn't. The first hundred days of any business have their discouragements and there was nobody hankering for the opportunity of financing my jazz band—not after I got myself fired because I couldn't jazz!

However, I managed to borrow a few hundred dollars on personal credit to guarantee my employees' salaries. What I could scrape together wasn't enough to guarantee any salary for myself, though, and so in those days I learned a good deal about plain living and high thinking.

It was slow work collecting men, because I wanted only those who could realize what I was trying to do. I hardly knew myself, except that

I saw possibilities in the music if it could be put on a scored, trained basis. The usual jazz orchestra gang was no good for my purpose and neither were the more set-in-their-way symphony players. I needed musically trained youngsters who were ambitious, slightly discontented and willing to adventure a little.

In San Francisco band circles I became known as a sort of nut, I think. At any rate, all the men that other leaders couldn't handle because of freak or stubborn streaks came to me, as one nut to another, I suppose. Occasionally one of these did fit into my scheme exactly as if he had been created for it. At last I had seven men of spirit and enterprise.

Then the War broke out. We got the news in the midst of a rehearsal. And the rehearsal, of course, broke up. In the following twenty-four hours, I tried all recruiting stations within walking distance and got turned down. In spite of recent thin living, I weighed almost three hundred pounds and the rules said I was no good for "combatant purposes."

After much argument, Washington ruled that I

could enlist as a band leader and I finally put on a Navy uniform, especially made. I had lost my seven picked men, but the Navy offered plenty of material for experimentation. Best of all, we had discipline, so that the trombonist couldn't get off practice whenever he had been out late the night before and the French horn never dared pipe a word about headaches.

Though I led a band, I had plenty of superior officers, too, and I learned something about being disciplined as well as disciplining. I was paid forty-two dollars a month and got it a good deal more regularly than later when I was paying other men forty times that.

At that, it was a grilling sort of life, and after I was out, I was all nerves. I was short of funds, too, and so there was no chance of starting my own orchestra again. As a stop-gap, I took charge of the Fairmont Hotel orchestra in San Francisco. I would direct a punchy number and then I would go out of sight and cry for ten minutes. This went on until I lost exactly a hundred pounds, falling off in three months from 285 to 185. When I went to a doctor, he told me to stop work and worry.

I told him I had a fat chance. It looked to me as if I'd be worrying until I died. And right here, perhaps it is all right for me to say that there is a good deal of truth in the old proverb that it is never darker than just before dawn. I am not much on the Pollyanna stuff, but after all, I have known what it was to lose my ambition and my nerve and my health—and find them all again.

There I was, a symphony player determined to break into something that the best people then considered the lowest of the low. It didn't look as if I had much chance to get anywhere, did it? Or jazz, either, for that matter. Yet not long before in New York, if I had only known it, something had happened that showed the mango magic was working.

The original Dixieland Jazz Band had come East and been hired by the Reisenweber Café. Up to then, New York had not heard any jazz. Chicago and New Orleans had, and San Francisco, but not New York, where after all, modes are made. Reisenweber's made something of a point of the band's début—raised the cover charge and boosted the food prices. The dancers came, too, but when they heard the music, they didn't know what to make of it.

The band played an entire jazz selection. Not a soul stepped out on the floor. The café manager, standing on the side-lines, was ready to weep with wretchedness. The men guests were suddenly conscious of their high collars and the women of shoes that hurt. And there sat the unhappy band, banging away, surrounded by a scene as festive as a funeral.

Finally the manager, desperate, dry-lipped, but determined, raised an arm to halt the incomprehensible music.

"This is jazz, ladies and gentlemen," he pleaded. "It's to be danced to."

Perhaps it was his woe-begone countenance that relieved the strain. At any rate, somebody laughed and every gentleman grabbed his lady and began to cavort. Bang, bang, slap bang, hip hooray! Jazz had hit New York and New York had gone down before it.

In two years the thing had sprung from New

Orleans to Chicago, from Chicago to San Francisco, had taken rough form and overrun the continent, had captured New York and spread from North to South and from East to West with only isolated portions of New England and New Englandism holding out against it.

III

Growing Pains

III: Growing Pains

A REPORTER who came once to get a success story from me complained that I hadn't undergone enough hardships to make me worth writing about. He explained that to be of any real value for his kind of tale, I should have gone to work at twelve to support an invalid mother and fourteen small sisters and brothers of assorted sizes. Another thing he deplored was that I hadn't "fought my way up." In fact, he intimated that it seemed as if I had risen without a great deal of trouble and then promptly slid down again of my own accord. That was his far-from-flattering estimate of jazz and jazz players and he is not alone in it.

It is true that I have only been broke at intervals and that, even then, I might have called upon relatives for help if I had been so minded. But just the same, I feel as if jazz and I have come over some pretty rough roads together. We have had to fight for every inch of recognition we have ever had, and folks have never spared our feelings if they felt inclined to tell us what they thought of us. They still consider us fair targets, as far as that goes. Every day or so, somebody emphasizes my horrible jazz present by referring to my honorable symphony and string-quartet past.

I am less vulnerable to such digs now that I'm standing on my own legs with a clear idea of what I am trying to do. And I don't mind admitting that having the price of a good-sized meal in my pocket adds a lot to my self-confidence. You can't get away from human nature—at least I can't—and I have no patience with the idea that art and starvation are twin sisters.

It's quite all right to starve for an ideal if you've got to, but in America you don't starve long if the ideal is worth starving for, in the first place. There is no country in the world where the common people, so-called, reward sincerity and honest effort in any line as lavishly as ours do. In that respect, it's a case of America's virtue being her own punishment, for it seems to be the fashion in certain high-brow groups to say contemptuously that we haven't any artists because none of them is starving.

What the jazz group is trying to do may prove in the long run to be worth while, or it may not. Only time will show. The point I am trying to make is that we believe in jazz. We didn't chuck our honorable places among honorable musicians just to go out after the filthy lucre, not by several tinker's dams. We claim we're still musicians, perhaps even better musicians than we would have been if we hadn't strayed off the straight and narrow paths allotted by convention to first-rate members of our profession.

At the same time, I want to make it clear that the financial side of recognition means just as much to me as it does to any man. I stand a good deal firmer on my legs, because, when I slap my pocket, I can hear a reassuring jangle of coin in it.

There was a sorry time when legs and pockets gave out all at once. That was after the War when I broke down at the Fairmont and had to give up my orchestra and take to bed for several months. For a while, then, I really did debate whether I hadn't better give up and let the I-told-you-so's, who said jazz would bring me to no good end, have it their own way.

I didn't, but when I finally got well, I hadn't a penny and was warned by my doctor not to take on much responsibility or hard work for a while. I finally set out to build up a band at the Potter Hotel in Santa Barbara. My old pre-war men were too expensive to be thought of in this new venture, so I had to make my new start with raw recruits.

These came chiefly from the high school. Bright, ambitious, nice youngsters they were, thrilled about jazz and eager to learn. The trouble was, not one of them had been taught to read music. Our rehearsals had to be conducted by ear and I had to build my boys into my musical idea without a trace of musical foundation. It was like making writers of free verse out of children who didn't know the alphabet. When a lad who could read notes applied for a job, I hailed him as manna from heaven, and he turned out to be the worst of the lot. He knew no more about music than a parrot knows about grammar.

Those untrained children, with their eager desire

to learn, made me realize what could be done by the schools if they would only take hold. Why is it that wealthy patrons of music will pour out millions for symphonies and not a cent for music in the public schools? It's my idea that every child ought to go to school with books under one arm and a horn or some other instrument under the other. Music—that is, music that they play themselves— arouses the interest of boys and girls alike, and is sure, I believe, to make the bad ones good and the good ones better.

From what I have seen, it seems to me that most music teachers must be teaching music as Latin teachers teach Latin—as though it were a dead language, something without any meaning in real life, something to be learned by rote. Music is a language all right but a living, changing, vital language. The solemn respect some people give it belongs only to things dead and canonized.

One of those Santa Barbara boys, a little chap who played the cornet, once woke me out of a sound sleep at 4 o'clock in the morning because he had forgotten how a difficult scoring ran. He was so interested that he didn't seem to think of apologizing for his unceremonious call, taking it for granted that I would feel just as he did about the urgency of the situation. He said he couldn't sleep for thinking of the music, so he got up and walked five miles to reach first aid.

Probably he didn't wake me up, anyway, for I was losing considerable sleep myself just then over the conditions that were making it impossible for me to carry out my plans for an experimental orchestra. Hardly a day passed that I didn't get some new idea for scoring or instrumentation, but I didn't have and couldn't get an adequate laboratory for testing my inventions. The more I worked with jazz, the surer I was that its authentic vitality would take root and develop on what I called a symphonic basis. I was longing to try it, anyway. A painter must feel like that when he is confronted with an extraordinarily paintable subject and there are no brushes in reach.

Saving money became suddenly a passion with me—spendthrift that I had always been. I wanted to save now because I wanted to be able to afford a good orchestra. For a while I led a sort of wandering minstrel life, directing orchestras in Pasa-

dena, Los Angeles, and San Francisco as opportunity came.

It was at the Maryland Hotel in Pasadena that
I was presented to the king of the Belgians, who
requested that I be brought up after he had heard us
play. It was the first time I had ever been introduced to royalty and I got all mixed up on what
to call him. Ever since, I have been afraid that I
addressed him as "king," but I have never dared
ask anybody.

He was very gracious, anyway, and asked some
questions about certain of the queer noises—meaning the saxophone and clarinet effects. I explained
as best I could, getting sort of red and flustered,
and then he said I should come to Europe sometime and play, and somebody mercifully led me
away to a corner where I could mop my brow in
peace and wonder just how many bones I had
pulled.

Intent on making as much money as I could as
quickly as possible, I joined a group which played
for dancing at the beach hotels on a the-dancer-
pays-the-fiddler plan. We musicians were equipped
with a big can into which our patrons threw dollars

Jazz

in return for jazz. At first this made me miserably ashamed, for I felt as if I were acting the cap-holding monkey for the hand-organ grinder on a street corner. But my need for money was so great just then that, when I saw the coins pouring in, I abandoned my scruples.

We players walked about among the crowd, and when one piece was finished, we waited for some-body to feed the can before we started another.

The movie folks were good customers—so good that we often allowed credit to the more reliable ones, including Charlie Chaplin. When they were dancing with someone they liked, they would hold up their fingers to indicate how much they were willing to pay to have the dance prolonged. We followed them around with our eyes and, as long as they'd continue to hold up fingers from time to time, we would continue to play. We enjoyed it and if some little girl from the provinces was dancing with a movie hero, she certainly did, too.

Once it cost an Iowa grocer sixty dollars to keep a certain film vamp for six dances. People began to drop away from the floor at the fourth dance without a pause between. During the fifth, only a few couples still hung on and when we were going fervently on into the sixth, the last of them puffed off the floor and still the Iowan danced on. It was before the days of cutting in, so he was safe enough as long as his wind held out—but he was fat, and perhaps thrift began to stir in the back of his mind, for during the sixth he held up no more fingers. When we stopped, he came breathless off the floor and we tackled him for our money. He tried to shade the price until one of our number basely suggested that perhaps he would rather have us send the bill back to his home town. Then he came through.

It wasn't pretty, but it was certainly life— absurd, ridiculous, chaotic, full of vigor, change, excitement and battle. Meantime, I was slowly piling up some money and hanging on doggedly to my ambition. But if it hadn't been for John Hernan, I'm not sure I'd have held out. Hernan, a California hotel man, was the first person who ever believed in me and my jazz enough to risk money on his belief.

One day when I was feeling blue, he came up to me.

"Think you could make good with a real or-chestra if you got the chance?" he asked me casually.

"Aw, what's the use of talking?" I muttered, not even looking at him. "I haven't got the chance."

"How do you know?" he shot back, and there was something in his voice that woke hope in me. I grabbed him by the arm just as he was pretending to walk off.

"What do you mean?" I begged, and I expect I hurt his arm with the grip I had on it.

"Well," said he, preparing to dodge thanks by fleeing round the corner, "I've just guaranteed your salary for a month to the management of the Alex-andria in Los Angeles. You start the thirteenth."

Another time that "thirteenth" might have given me superstitious pause, but this was one occasion that I didn't even think of it. We did open on the thirteenth, too, and I'll never forget that first night if I live to be a million years old.

Word had got about among some of my friends in the movies that I was making my début at the Alexandria. They rallied full force for the occa-sion, all dressed up and in joyful mood. They clapped and we played on and on and on—better than we had ever played at rehearsal, better, I sometimes think, than we have ever played since.

I guess some of the crowd must have gone out between dances and telephoned friends to come on over, because couples kept pouring in. I can see them all now—Charlie Chaplin solemnly burlesquing my conducting while everybody roared, Pauline Frederick, Mabel Normand, gayest and prettiest of all, Harold Lloyd, Cecil de Mille—but it would take a blue book of the films to list them all.

You see, in spite of the stories you hear about its illicit gayety, Hollywood gets pretty dull of evenings and the stars were glad enough to have something new to do. Wallace Reid was there, I remember, and played the drum with the orchestra. He often came in after that to try out the drum or saxophone. We were always glad when he chose the saxophone because it was easier drowned out. Poor Wallie was a fine fellow and a splendid actor, but not much of a drummer or saxophonist.

Of course, we were pleased that the first night went off so well, but we knew we weren't out of the woods yet by a long shot, so the next day and the next and the next, we tried harder and harder. I suppose I must have slept some during that time, but I can't remember any periods of sweet, dreamless ease. Our first-night customers stayed with us and so many more came that, at the end of the month, John Hernan was told we had made good and would be kept. At the close of the year, symphonic jazz had proved so successful that the Alexandria's cover receipts had risen from $300 to $1200 a day.

It would seem that I should have been earning plenty of money by this time, but I was not. Starting on a shoestring as I had, we adopted the coöperative plan in the orchestra. I was to have the largest share of the proceeds. That was all right as far as it went, but the difficulty was that whenever one of my men threatened to accept a better offer, I had to take something off my own salary to keep him satisfied.

One day a fellow came up with a telegram. Without a word, he handed it to me and I read an offer from another leader at $25 more than he was getting.

"Well?" he prompted, when I didn't speak.

The reason I didn't speak was that I was figuring how much I could cut down on what I was keeping for myself and still eat regularly. He was a good man and I wanted to be fair with him. Finally I said: "Will a thirty dollar raise be all right?"

He said it would and hurried off, jubilant. That week and for many weeks following, I paid him thirty dollars of my own money—until one day I found he had faked the telegram. He hadn't even had another offer.

The men averaged $100 a week. I got sometimes as little as $40 and felt myself lucky. Indeed, for a time after I was leading a successful jazz orchestra and getting a lot of publicity for it, I was barely scraping by from week to week.

It was not until much later, when we began to make records, that dissatisfaction arose among the men over the coöperative system and we gave it up. It wasn't very fair. For instance, in making a record, the drummer, who might strike his cymbal once in an entire number, got the same as the man who played five or six instruments and worked every second of the time. After that, I paid each man a straight salary, varying according to his ability and usefulness. And from that time, I began to make some real money for myself.

For quite a while I did the arrangements and orchestrations, as well as the conducting, but it was too much for one man, so we took on Ferdie Grofe, talented symphony player and composer. Now the two of us work out our ideas together.

The chance for the orchestra (or band, as we called it then), to go East, came when the Ambassador Hotel at Atlantic City was opened. S. W. Straus agreed to lend us the money to make the trip. He gambled to the extent of $2,600 on us. But it was all right. We made good and he got his money back.

Until we went to Atlantic City, the only recognition we had won, aside from the approval of those who danced to our music, came from persons interested in our trick of jazzing the classics—that is, of applying our peculiar treatment of rhythm and color to well-known masterpieces.

The notice this brought us was not always of the pleasantest. Certain correspondents called us scoundrels and desecrators and one man described us as ghouls "bestializing the world's sweetest harmonies," rather a mixed metaphor, it seemed to me. A woman with a gift of epithet termed us "vultures, devouring the dead masters."

I don't get mad at these communications and I always read them. Sometimes I can even see justice in them. Besides, it's good to know the worst that people think of us. But of course I don't agree that we have done such very terrible things to the classics. I don't think we've even insulted them much.

I worship certain of the classics myself and respect them all. But I doubt if it hurts Tschaikowsky or even Bach when we rearrange what they have written—provided we choose appropriate compositions of theirs—and play to people who haven't heard good music before.

I have never had the feeling that I must keep my hands off the "dead masters," as people feel they must not speak the truth of the dead unless it is a complimentary truth. The masters are not dead to me. I think of the great writers of music, not as gods who finished their jobs forever in seven days, but as plain human men, as human as any of the rest of us. They were working on a job that will never be finished as long as human beings live, for music is as much a part of life as the heart beat. Every human being has music in him if he would realize it and let it out. The masters had genius where probably, at the very best, I have only talent; but they didn't care a bit more about beauty than I do or try any harder to capture it. And they didn't scruple to take any material they could lay their hands on to help them, either.

You remember the verse of Kipling's:

"When 'Omer smote 'is bloomin' lyre,
    'E'd 'eard men sing by land and sea;
An' what 'e thought 'e might require,
    'E went an' took, the same as me."

Not that I mean to imply that there was any real musical value in our jazzing the classics. Of course not. It was partly a trick and partly experimental work. We were just fooling around with the nearest material, working out our methods.

The old masters are not the best material we can use. A jazz orchestra is better off when playing scores that have been written expressly for it. By degrees we are accumulating a library of our own music. But that's another story to which I shall return later.

The prospect of the trip East frightened even while it thrilled us. California was home to most of us and while the folks there hammered us occasionally, they also humored us. We might be wild, but we were theirs and they were fond of us. The effete East—we always spoke of the East as effete—had no personal interest in us and might do worse than scorn—it might ignore us.

So we were nervously uneasy as we swung aboard the transcontinental express bound for New York and points East. Atlantic City was like a new world—a world we didn't like so very well at first. Indeed, after a few weeks of it, the boys begged to go back to the Coast.

The golden sunshine and the whole-hearted camaraderie of California had taken on increased enchantment as the distance between us widened. My gang didn't think folks were very friendly in Atlantic City and they claimed the Atlantic Ocean was vastly inferior to the Pacific. Even the neckties in the shops were sadly lacking in pep, they complained. In short, they were good and homesick.

Moreover, the Ambassador Hotel was out of the beaten track, being far up the Boardwalk and we were newcomers, unknown to the East, so patronage did not exactly rush our way.

I've always maintained it was a girl who finally started us on the road to popularity. I don't know her name or where she came from. All we have ever known about her is that she had yellow hair and brown eyes and danced like a wood nymph. One listless, gloomy day when we were playing for a handful of people, she walked into the room with a typical masculine tea hound. She was bored and showed it. He tried to make conversation and she pouted.

Then the music started. They danced, and to our delight, she began as the trombonist put it, "to snap out of it." We all felt an interest in her. The next day she came again, bringing a whole tableful. After that, she rarely missed an afternoon and she was always accompanied by a large party. Business fairly bounced out of its depression. We never spoke to the girl nor she to us, but we knew she was press-agenting us all over town. We certainly were grateful, too.

Even though we eventually did well at the Ambassador and began to pay Mr. Straus back, we might have gone home if the Victor Phonograph Company had not held a convention at Atlantic City. A representative of theirs, Calvin Childs, happened to lunch at the Ambassador and heard us play.

After that, I felt as if I were being rushed for a fraternity at college. Childs came up and fervently insisted that we do nothing about a phonograph contract until he had time to communicate with his firm. Only six of our men had come East and I suggested that he wait until he could hear us all.

"We sound much better full force," I apologized.

"Nonsense," he incredibly responded, "you can't be much better than you are now. 'S not possible!"

And a few days afterward, we got a nice, fat two-year contract. That was the beginning of so many unbelievable cyclonic happenings that we began to get used to miracles. The Palais Royal, largest café in New York City, waved a contract at us. Vaudeville scouts approached us. Our pictures were in the papers. Sometimes, of course, things still went awfully wrong; but on the whole, we were in good danger of getting our heads turned.

To the Palais Royal came all the country's great names and foreign visitors of renown, too. Any night at all, we could look out and see Vanderbilts, Drexel Biddles, Goulds and the rest dancing to our music. Lord and Lady Mountbatten, cousins of the Prince of Wales, were among the distinguished guests one night. They had just arrived in this country to spend their honeymoon.

After that night, they came often, for they adored dancing. They were such a friendly, jolly pair that when they were in the room, we invariably played almost nothing but their favorite pieces. We had many conversations, and Lord Mountbatten got to be friends with every boy in the band.

"You've simply got to come to London," he kept saying. "The Prince must have a chance to hear the band—that's all there is to it."

And after the pair had gone back to London, there came a letter with crests and coronets on its seal, telling us again that we must come to London where Lord Mountbatten himself "wanted the pleasure of presenting us to the Prince."

Part of the result of our New York vogue was

that smart hostesses began to want us for private parties. The first of these, at the home of a very rich, very well-known New Yorker, was almost a fizzle. Up to this time, we had played for private parties only in California, where nearly everybody knew us. There we were all fairly prosperous, with small cars of our own, well-fitting tuxedos and no idea at all that anybody was better than we were. So, while we played for the guests for pay, we always ate in the dining room and received the same consideration from the host that any visitor to his house would get.

But the East, it seemed, was to be different. Orchestras were hired by the social secretary to play for an entertainment and then turned over to the butler to look after. So when I got to the house in question on the night we were to play there, I found all the men out in the street.

"What's up?" I asked amazed.

"Well," said the biggest sax player, " we didn't know what you would want us to do. They told us, when we rang the front doorbell, to go round to the servants' entrance. We aren't going."

I went to the front door and obtained an audience with the rather flustered and embarrassed host.

"My men don't wear second-hand tuxedos nor eat with their knives and they are a good deal like gentlemen," I told him casually.

After that, we were always treated just as we had been in California.

Into the midst of our already busy days, about this time came a contract for a season with the Ziegfeld Follies. The first night we played with them was one of the most miserable I ever spent.

We were seated on a platform designed to move forward. When the time came for it to start, it didn't. We had stage fright, anyway, and the failure of the mechanism to move on schedule fairly froze the smiles on our faces. We played on, but I thought we sounded worse than the worst dress rehearsal we had ever had. And then, when we weren't expecting it, the platform gave a leap like a skittish colt, flinging us forward and almost knocking our teeth down our throats.

I thought, of course, we were a flop and wouldn't even read the papers the next day. But to my surprise, I heard they spoke not so badly of us and the next night we got on fine, platform and all.

New York is a queer city. I have the theory that novelty, not luck or ability is what gets by there. New York doesn't care about merit so much as it does about something new to tickle its eyes, its palate or its ears. The newspapers reflect this. It is a city of press agents and I used to wonder how they all lived.

"It's easy enough," one told me, "New York city editors like press agents who produce the goods. They don't want you to pretend with them, but if you have a story, that is different; they will give you the front page any time."

The bizarre and the unusual get not only the headlines, but the homage and shekels. Naturally, anything new has always an army of imitators and soon one's vogue wears out. There is nothing real or lasting in novelty alone.

We realized that to New York we were just a novelty at a dull season, something to make the great city stop, look, listen and dance for the time. We had a hankering to be taken seriously. We even believed that there was something worth-while about jazz—danceable, as it was. We were doing the best we could with it and once in a while there was the satisfaction of hearing a flapper humming really good music without knowing it was good—something we had "sold" her.

But no one took us seriously. At that stage, it wouldn't have done to say anything about jazz being an art, even a lively one. The artistic would merely have scoffed and the flapper and her beaux would have looked sheepish at being accused of a liking for anything that was highbrow. Altogether, I thought it would be a good time to get out of New York for a while. And since I had seen, as everybody must see, the American adoration for the European, I played with the idea of going abroad. I knew singers, nice American boys and girls, who were unable to get a hearing in their own country until they had studied in Italy or France. They were not particularly improved by the European period that I could see. On the contrary they usually lost something—whatever it was that made them distinctive. But the point was, they had gained what the public seemed to want them to have—foreign flavor. Especially if they returned wearing a foreign name.

I figured that my orchestra would probably get more serious consideration for what was in the back of my head to do, if we obtained a little of the foreign stamp for ourselves. And we wouldn't need to bring back any Russian prefixes or French suffixes, either.

The end of it was that we sailed for Europe, March 3, 1923, on the *S. S. President Harding*, American line. We were a strictly American bunch. Most of us had never been abroad. Wild Westerners all, we had managed to adapt ourselves to Broadway, but Europe was something else again.

There was a terrified lump in my throat as the Statue of Liberty curtsied out of sight. I had a premonition we might better have stayed at home. The boys, though, were excited and confident.

"Lookut what we did to New York," one encouraged me, as I was loudly proclaiming on a very seasick day that I wished we hadn't come. I was risking $18,000 of my own money on the trip and, in spite of the fabulous salary the newspapers credited me with receiving, that much ready cash looked mighty big to me, especially as I had got married in New York and was learning what it costs a lady to shop on Fifth Avenue.

The moment our ship dropped anchor at Liverpool, it seemed that my premonition had not been groundless. Our coming had been heralded, and the British Ministry of Labor was waiting for us. We had been engaged to play in "Brighter London," a revue at the Hippodrome, and the matter of labor permits had been, we thought, fixed up.

Now, however, we found we had another guess coming. The Ministry of Labor had an idea we had better not land. We were finally allowed to set foot on English soil, but were told we would not be allowed to play, so to speak, in English air. The matter became, in a way, international. We cabled our own Secretary of Labor to help us out, and the politico-legal tangle grew more than jazzy. England objected to us, so far as I could make out, on the ground that, if American jazz was once heard in England, tens of thousands of English musicians, unable to play it, would be thrown out of employment. Our success was taken for granted, which was very flattering, and I could only hope that the belief was based on the fact that some member or members of the Labor Commission had heard us play. But flattery wasn't much comfort if we were to be sent home unheard.

At length we were given permission to play in "Brighter London," but were denied the right to take the orchestra to a restaurant or supper club. Finally we got around that restriction, too, by hiring the same number of English musicians as we had Americans, and were allowed to play at Grafton Galleries, a night club. Our recruits never seemed to get the hang of jazz, though. There was something about it that was perfectly foreign to them. Perhaps they took it too seriously. But since that was what I had been praying for—seriousness in considering it—I suppose I shouldn't have minded that.

I remember one day asking one of my English musicians, "Can you ad lib?" Perhaps I should mention that "ad lib" is a jazz musical term meaning to improvise, to invent as you go along.

"Certainly," answered the man, rather nettled, "I can ad lib anything."

"Then do it," I requested.

"All right, just write something for me to ad lib," he agreed.

Orchestra leaders used to come to our rehearsals, bringing their men, and we were glad to show them what we could. They played beautifully, too, so long as they could imitate. Give them a perfectly scored jazz orchestration and they could do it so well that it sounded like the real thing. But when it came to originating, they fell down. Jazz was simply not in their blood. They lacked the spontaneity, the exuberance, the courage—I do not know what. The something, whatever it is we call American, the indefinable something that is jazz. They didn't have it and it isn't something that can be put on the outside like a plaster. Most of the jazz orchestras that have since sprung up in London have failed simply because of that fact.

There was plenty of opposition to us, even apart from the labor trouble. "Why should a man check his mentality with his hat at the door?" inquired a distinguished British organist, when somebody tried to bring him to hear us play at supper. And many felt the same way.

The most unsuccessful benefit I ever played in

my life was one at Albert Hall for the air service hospitals. In the first place, my band of twelve pieces followed one of seventy. The place was too big for us and I am sure we did sound awful. Just the same, we were hardly prepared to have the man who had asked us to play the benefit come up afterwards and tell us it was positively the worst band he had ever heard. Still, that's usually the way of benefits. People seldom appreciate what they get for nothing.

We had a good time in London, though, and after they got over their prejudices, some of the Londoners seemed to like us. Certainly we liked them. I was especially fond of their bathtubs, the largest I have ever seen. And their bobbies, or policemen, that are bigger still.

One day I saw a huge bobby calmly lift one of those tiny English cars right out of the road when it came farther than he had directed it. Another time, Mrs. Whiteman was driving down Bond Street and happened to see a coat she liked in a shop window. She almost forgot her wheel in her effort to see the price tag.

The bobby at the crossing called out, "What's the matter?"

"Oh, I'm sorry," she told him, "I was just trying to see the price of that coat in the window."

He turned toward the window. "The green one? Well, it's forty guineas. Now drive along, madam." And all with a wide smile.

We were introduced to the autograph habit in London. I never knew we had it here until recently, when everybody seems to have got the bug. But in England, they appear always to have had it. People carry fat little books into the subway, theater and street, stopping persons they happen to recognize.

Once I was unwittingly a source of income to some sharp little English messenger boys. A small girl stopped me as I was leaving the Hippodrome and when I finished writing my name for her, some people came running over from a queue forming at a theater on the other side of the street. I wrote my name until my arm ached and suddenly I realized that the same two urchins were coming back again and again. They were selling the autographs for a penny apiece to the queue.

76

The orchestra played at Grafton Galleries every evening after the performance at the Hippodrome and often we were honored by the patronage of the Prince of Wales. The first time I saw his Royal Highness, however, was about a week after we landed. True to his promise, Lord Mountbatten gave a party for the Prince and asked us to play. There were just thirty-two guests, all related to the throne and it was the nicest party I ever went to. There was no swank and no ostentation. The guests were all simple, cordial people who knew how to enjoy themselves.

The Prince had already arrived when I went into the room, but I was so nervous that I couldn't tell him from any of the others. I had a bad attack of stage fright and I wished I were somewhere else. Lord Mountbatten was disgusted with me. He is such a democratic, unassuming chap himself that he can't imagine anybody getting into what he calls a "funk" over a mere meeting with a prince.

"What on earth shall I call him?" I wanted to know, distractedly.

Lord Mountbatten looked at me disappointedly. "Why, you aren't a British subject," he reminded me. "What do you call anybody? Just be natural."

I hope I was natural, but if I wasn't at first, I was later; for the Prince put me instantly at ease with some flattering comment about the orchestra. He was wearing evening clothes and I thought I had never seen a man's shoulders look better in such dress. The Prince of Wales is really rather small, but for some reason, partly the way he carries himself, I suppose, you never realize it, even in his pictures.

I saw him many times after that evening. Sometimes we played for parties he or others gave at private houses; and whenever he wanted me, instead of sending an equerry to "command" my presence, he would come himself and ask in friendly fashion if it would be convenient for us to play.

We never accepted any pay from him. He insisted upon it many times, but I told him we had come to London mostly to play for him and considered it honor enough to have that privilege. We did, too, and it wasn't altogether because he was a prince. Everybody does things for him because they like him so much, and I believe, if he were

Jazz Welcoming Jazz Back from Europe

just plain John Smith, he would still have the winning personality that gets favor for its owner everywhere. I am sure of one thing—if the world were choosing a king, the Prince of Wales would win the crown by popular acclaim.

As a host, he was splendid. The first night we played for him, I caught my drummer rushing out of the house.

"What on earth's the matter?" I called, worried.

"I'm goin' to cable my old man that the Prince of Wales served me champagne with his own hands," he shouted back.

The reason the Prince did not entertain at York House where he lives is that he keeps bachelor's hall there. So when he wants to give a party, he must borrow a house somewhere.

His Royal Highness is an extraordinarily good dancer, I should say, with a splendid sense of rhythm. Perhaps that is one reason he likes the drum so much—for its rhythm. He told me he got his first drum when he was four and immediately learned to beat it under the tutelage of some old soldier around the palace. It is not strange that royalty should be captivated by the drum, for their entire lives are measured by its beats. When they are born, the drums are beaten to tell the story. When they are married the drum comes into play again, and when they have an heir or go to war or die.

The drummer with our orchestra explained all his tricks to his Royal Highness and claimed also to have learned a special rat-a-tat from his pupil. The papers always play up any preference of the Prince so energetically that I think he sometimes feels he will never again say what he does like. He did confess, though, that he is fond of the ukelele and the bagpipes. He learned to play the pipes at Oxford and there is a story that his friends (for he was a regular good fellow and into all the life of the school) stole into his room one night and pricked the air from his favorite bags because they got so tired of hearing him practice. They also changed his title to the "Prince of Wails."

We all addressed his Highness quite informally as Prince. He once remarked upon this habit of Americans who, he says, Prince him until he feels like barking. The quality I liked most in young Edward Albert was his consideration for others. I

saw a hundred instances of it with his personal at-
tendants and others who served him. He noticed
that a saxophonist was absent one night and asked
solicitously if he were ill. When next he saw the
man, he remembered to inquire all about his grippe.

I have never seen such a memory for everything
—facts, names and faces—as the Prince has. It
was after I came back to America that he visited
Canada. I sent him a message asking him to the
re-opening of the Palais Royal. He couldn't come
and later, when he reached New York, the first
thing he said to me was: "I was mighty sorry I
couldn't come to your opening, but I was way up
on my ranch and didn't get your message until too
late to make it."

The orchestra members were all delighted when
Clarence Mackay, arranging a great ball in his
Highness's honor, asked us to play. That was a
gorgeous party—the beautiful Mackay estate on
Long Island, with its flowers and lights and the
prettiest women in the country decked in their finest
gowns and jewels. We were counted three times on
our way into the house, the last time by Mr.
Mackay himself. Guards were everywhere and the

invitation cards were watched as if they had been jewels, for it was a safe bet that a lot of the city's "celebrity hunters" would try to force their way in. The Prince, on the occasion of this, his second visit, had become more popular and more interesting than ever, so that he was not allowed even breathing time away from watching eyes. But Mr. Mackay was determined he should have at least one partly undisturbed evening.

As far as that went, the guests at the ball were almost as interested in the royal guest's movements as the outside world was. Every time he came on the dancing floor, there was a sound like the catching of breath and every woman there watched him with wistful eyes. For of course, he might, just might, ask her to dance.

He was his usual pleasant self with us and several times asked for favorite pieces to be played. He also asked me if I would send him the record of the "Rhapsody in Blue."

Of course, this is really getting ahead of my story, for the visit of the Prince to this country the second time and the party at the Mackays' all came after my return from London. We came back

really because we got homesick. Funny—we had
a wonderful time in England and when we had
been in New York and thinking of ourselves as
Westerners, we hadn't cared so much for the East.
But in London, we suddenly began to feel that
Broadway was superior to Bond Street or the Rue de
la Paix or any other street we had ever seen.

We had some good offers to stay in London and
a group of capitalists in Paris wanted to build a
theater for us if we would come over there. But
we had been working hard for a long time on an
enterprise that was as close to my heart as home
itself, and I wanted to get back to New York and
try it out.

All this time, you see, we had been testing, discarding and endeavoring to get volume with the
instruments we had, and trying also for harmony
and sweetness. We weren't quite ready for the
experiment I wanted and yet dreaded to spring, but
I thought we needed the American atmosphere
for rehearsals. So we sailed back again to America.
And if you'll believe it, all was quite as I had
dreamed it might be. New York received us with
open arms—gave us a great reception, as if we'd

been distinguished foreigners coming on a visit.

We caught sight of Liberty and of airplanes filled with bands almost at the same minute. They serenaded us from the air, from the water and from land. The Mayor sent a representative down the Bay to meet us and so did the Police Department.

That night at the Waldorf they gave us a dinner —a dinner with speeches by all sorts of personages —and such a greeting that we couldn't believe they meant us at all. When they asked me to make a response, I found tears rolling down my cheeks.

It is a great thing, after a long hard struggle, to find success and appreciation. For a moment, I forgot any cynicism I had felt about the false value of the European label in America. Cynicism doesn't take deep root in an American, anyway. I only felt happy, touched, almost overcome by the warm-hearted generosity of our welcome home. It seemed to me then that everybody understood me, that my orchestra was a real success, that there was nothing in the future but sunshine and roses. But even at that moment, I didn't forget that we had come home to do bigger things in jazz than had ever been done before. If we could.

IV

An Experiment

IV: An Experiment

*V*ISIONS of playing a jazz concert in what a critic has called the "perfumed purlieus" of Aeolian Hall, used to rouse me up at night in a cold perspiration. Sometimes a nightmare depicted me being borne out of the place on a rail, and again I dreamed the doors were all but clattering down with the applause.

That's the way I lived during waking hours, too, all the time I was planning the Aeolian Hall experiment—alternating between extremes of dire fear and exultant confidence.

We began to rehearse for the concert as soon as we came back from England. The idea struck nearly everybody as preposterous at the start. Some hold to the same opinion still. But the list of pessimists was a little shorter, I believe, when at half-past five, on the afternoon of February 12, 1924, we took our fifth curtain call.

J a z z

"What! an all-jazz concert?" one of my best friends, a musician, shouted when I confided my plan to him in strictest secrecy. "Why, my boy, it simply can't be done. You mustn't try it. It would ruin you! You have your future to think of—and your reputation. So far you've been getting on splendidly with your dance music and if you watch your step, you will undoubtedly be able to put away a good smart sum while the vogue lasts. But a jazz concert! Honestly, my boy, I'm afraid you've got softening of the brain. Be guided by me in this and you will never regret it."

Such expressions were naturally depressing, especially since I myself realized that I was gambling with public favor. There were plenty of similar warnings from other friends and those who weren't in that category said even worse things. I was called "fresh," "publicity-hungry," "money-mad" —and some of the musicians I most admired, who had until then regarded me with a slightly amused but tolerant air, now talked themselves red in the face about the insolence of jazz boys who want to force their ridiculous efforts upon the world—by the world meaning, I suppose, their own little coterie, the final court of critical appeal in their opinion.

Here's something I have never been able to understand. Why should it be supposed that all the good taste in the world is monopolized by a few people? Isn't it possible that the so-called masses have considerable instinctive good judgment in matters of beauty that they never get credit for? My notion is that beauty is for everybody, that anything too precious for the common gaze is out of place in a world God has created for ordinary people. That's why I resent the self-assurance of certain high and mighty art circles.

However, it was not a time for me to start any arguments. And anyway, in spite of all my fine theories, I was mighty anxious to win the approval of the select few. It wouldn't be enough for me simply to gather into Aeolian Hall a capacity audience of flappers and dancing men. We had to have the musicians, the critics, the music students—the type of man who takes music seriously as vocation or avocation. Even the one who takes it solemnly —although that isn't at all my idea of the way it should be taken.

Jazz

It's extraordinary, when you think of it, how timid we all are about our own opinions. We may like something but we don't like it until we find that someone who is supposed to know says he likes it. I forget who said, "Stand a sheep on its hind legs and you do not have a man; but stand a flock of sheep on their hind legs and you have a crowd of men"; but he was nearly right. And deep down in each one of us there is, after all, something sheep-like. We hate to go in any direction until we look around to see if someone else has started that way.

So a great many people, in their timidity, smother their own natural tastes. This is especially true, it seems to me, in music. This idea that the arts are so high and fine that an ordinary common man can't really know anything about them is combined with our natural timidity. As long as the critics condemn a new musical development, the common man may like it, but he is shame-faced about it. "I don't know anything about music," he says. And most of the time he doesn't have the nerve to go ahead and add: "But I know what I like."

Now as a matter of fact, critics are just human

beings like anybody else. The only difference is that they aren't afraid to say that they know what they like. They have had opportunities to study a lot about what I may call the superstructure of music. They know technique and a whole language of musical terms. But the foundation of music— or any other art—is in human emotion. The common man who doesn't know counterpoint from harmony, may know what he likes—that is, what appeals to his deep, fundamental, human emotions —as well as any critic. In fact, he may know it better, because his musical education doesn't get in the way. His approach to music is more simple and direct. And in the history of art, it is a fact that only the art the common people have recognized and loved stands the test of time.

The American people ought to have more courage in their attitude toward the arts. Perhaps then they would realize that their own opinions about music have some importance. Or perhaps they might if they knew a little about how critics are made—and musicians, too, for that matter.

Some people seem to think I've climbed upon some high mountain peak of importance just because I'm one of the leaders of the new music. But what am I, when you come down to it? Just a Denver boy, who had some knowledge of musical technique pounded into me when I was a kid. I've spent my life learning more and more about technique, but I know no more about music, the deep meaning of the tone harmonies that arouse the depths of the human soul, than any man who responds to it.

And the critics—well, I know one in San Francisco who was a police reporter and probably never would have been a critic if the regular one hadn't been on his vacation one day when a concert was scheduled. The city editor sent the police reporter to report the concert and he turned in a good story. So when the regular critic quit, the police reporter was put on music. And now when that critic says a conductor is good, all San Francisco agrees with him.

A dramatic critic on a New York afternoon sheet was offered more money by a powerful morning combination and accepted precipitously. A rewrite man came in to work as usual that day and was assigned by the managing editor to cover an important play that night. With fear and trembling, but like the good soldier that a well-trained newspaper man always is, he went. The next day, he was appointed dramatic critic.

The point I'm making isn't that these men haven't sound opinions, worth listening to. They have. But what I want to say is that Denver boys who haven't grown up to conduct orchestras and police reporters who haven't got jobs as critics have sound opinions, too, and we ought to listen to them. When all the musicians and critics of to-day are dead and dust, it's the verdict of these ordinary, musically-uneducated men that will stand. It's their opinion that will determine whether or not we are remembered, just as, I'm bound to say, it was their opinion that kept "Abie's Irish Rose" running in New York for a record-breaking number of seasons after every critic in town had flayed it.

If I'd been willing to wait a few centuries for a verdict on my work, I wouldn't have been so wrought up over the Aeolian Hall concert. But here I saw the common people of America taking all the jazz they could get and mad to get more, yet not having the courage to admit that they took it seriously. I believed that jazz was beginning a new movement in the world's art of music. I wanted it to be recognized as such. I knew it never would be in my lifetime until the recognized authorities on music gave it their approval.

My idea for the concert was to show these skeptical people the advance which had been made in popular music from the day of discordant early jazz to the melodious form of the present. I believed that most of them had grown so accustomed to condemning the "Livery Stable Blues" sort of thing, that they went on flaying modern jazz without realizing that it was different from the crude early attempts—that it had taken a turn for the better.

My task was to reveal the change and try to show that jazz had come to stay and deserved recognition. It was not a light undertaking, but setting Aeolian Hall as the stage of the experiment was probably a wise move. It started the talk going, at least, and aroused curiosity. "Jazz in Aeolian Hall!" the conservatives cried incredulously. "What is the world coming to?"

An Experiment

While we were getting ready for the concert, we gave a series of luncheons for the critics, took them to rehearsals and explained painstakingly what we hoped to prove, at the same time displaying our orchestral tools for the enterprise. They were good sports and many offered helpful, though doubtful, encouragement.

That took one weight off my mind, for I saw that they were at least curious enough to come to the concert. But just the same, I was good and scared. We were trying to get a favorable hearing from the most hide-bound creatures in the world—educated musicians. It was educated musicians who scorned Wagner, resisted Debussy and roasted Chopin, you may remember. What, then, could we expect? Annihilation, perhaps.

I trembled at our temerity when we made out the lists of patrons and patronesses for the concert. But in a few days, I exulted at our daring, for the acceptances began to come in—from Damrosch, Godowsky, Heifetz, Kreisler, McCormack, Rachmaninoff, Rosenthal, Stokowski, Stransky. We had kindly response, too, from Alda, Galli-Curci, Garden, Gluck and Jeanne Gordon. Otto Kahn and Jules Glaenzer agreed to represent the patrons of art on our roster and the prominent writers we asked were equally obliging. These included: Fannie Hurst, Heywood Broun, Frank Crowninshield, S. Jay Kaufman, Karl Kitchin, Leonard Liebling, O. O. McIntyre, Pitts Sanborn, Gilbert Seldes, Deems Taylor and Carl Van Vechten.

Anybody who has breathlessly, almost unbelievingly, watched a precious ambition finally flower, will not think me maudlin when I confess that I used to pore over that list the way one does over a new picture of one's self, scanning it again and again for the mere pleasure of looking.

Perhaps I have emphasized what some readers may regard as the least important feature of the projected concert—the audience. But it was, after all, the main item, being uncertain. Before I began on it, I had the orchestra ready with a program I believed would launch our test adequately. I wasn't afraid of that angle. My boys had been playing what I called interesting music in a crowded restaurant where clattering dishes, staccato talk and laughter interfered with "reception," as the radio fans term it. At Aeolian Hall, the orchestra would have a fair chance to put over our musical message to a judicial few.

That concert cost $11,000. I lost about $7,000 on it. The program alone, together with the explanatory notes, cost $900. We rehearsed for many weeks and since it was outside our regular work, every rehearsal meant extra pay for the men. Nine musicians were added for the occasion and their salaries also piled up the total.

I didn't care. It would have been worth it to me at any price. But never in my life had I such stage fright as that day. I had no doubt of the orchestra. But how would people take it? Would we be the laughing-stock of the town when we woke the "morning after"? Would the critics decide I was trying to be smart and succeeding in being only smart-alecky? Or might I be able to convince the crowd that I was engaged in a sincere experiment, designed to exhibit what had been accomplished in the past few years with respect to scoring and arranging music for the popular band—that we were making a bona fide attempt to arouse an interest in popular music rhythm for purposes of advancing serious musical composition?

Fifteen minutes before the concert was to begin, I yielded to a nervous longing to see for myself what was happening out front, and putting an overcoat over my concert clothes, I slipped around to the entrance of Aeolian Hall.

There I gazed upon a picture that should have imparted new vigor to my wilting confidence. It was snowing, but men and women were fighting to get into the door, pulling and mauling each other as they do sometimes at a baseball game, or a prize fight, or in the subway. Such was my state of mind by this time, that I wondered if I had come to the right entrance. And then I saw Victor Herbert going in. It was the right entrance, sure enough, and the next day, the ticket office people said they could have sold out the house ten times over.

I went back stage again, more scared than ever. Black fear simply possessed me. I paced the floor, gnawed my thumbs and vowed I'd give $5,000 if we could stop right then and there. Now that the audience had come, perhaps I had really nothing to offer after all. I even made excuses to keep the curtain from rising on schedule. But finally there was no longer any way of postponing the evil moment. The curtain went up and before I could dash forth, as I was tempted to do, and announce that there wouldn't be any concert, we were in the midst of it.

It was a strange audience out in front. Vaudevillians, concert managers come to have a look at the novelty, Tin Pan Alleyites, composers, symphony and opera stars, flappers, cake-eaters, all mixed up higgledy-piggledy.

Beginning with the earliest jazz composition, "Livery Stable Blues," we played twenty-six selections designed to exhibit legitimate scoring as contrasted with the former hit and miss effects which were also called jazz. At that time I argued that all was not jazz that was so called. I still believe that "Livery Stable Blues" and "A Rhapsody in Blue," played at the concert by its talented composer, George Gershwin, are so many millions of miles apart, that to speak of them both as jazz needlessly confuses the person who is trying to understand modern American music. At the same time, in the course of a recent tour of the United States, I have become convinced that people as a whole like the word "jazz." At least they will have none of the

99

numerous substitutes that smart wordologists are continually offering. So I say, let's call the new music "jazz."

This, then, is the jazz program we played that day:

TRUE FORM OF JAZZ
    a. Ten years ago—"Livery Stable Blues"
    b. With Modern Embellishment—"Mama Loves Papa" .... *Baer*

COMEDY SELECTIONS
    a. Origin of "Yes, We Have No Bananas" .... *Silver*
    b. Instrumental Comedy—"So This Is Venice" .... *Thomas*
    (*Adapted from "The Carnival of Venice"*)

CONTRAST—LEGITIMATE SCORING VS. JAZZING
    a. Selection in True Form—
        "Whispering" .... *Schonberger*
    b. Same Selection with Jazz Treatment.....

RECENT COMPOSITIONS WITH MODERN SCORE
    a. "Limehouse Blues" .... *Braham*
    b. "I Love You" .... *Archer*
    c. "Raggedy Ann" .... *Kern*

An Experiment

ZEZ CONFREY (Piano)

    a. Medley Popular Airs ....

    b. "Kitten on the Keys" .... *Confrey*

    c. "Ice Cream and Art" ....

    d. "Nickel in the Slot" .... *Confrey*

         (*Accompanied by the Orchestra*)

FLAVORING A SELECTION WITH BORROWED
           THEMES

    "Russian Rose" .... *Grofe*

      (*Based on the Volga Boat Song*)

SEMI-SYMPHONIC ARRANGEMENT OF POPULAR
           MELODIES

Consisting of

    "Alexander's Ragtime Band" .... *Berlin*

    "A Pretty Girl Is Like a Melody".... *Berlin*

    "Orange Blossoms in California" ..... *Berlin*

A SUITE OF SERENADES .... *Herbert*

    a. Spanish

    b. Chinese

    c. Cuban

    d. Oriental

Jazz

ADAPTATION OF STANDARD SELECTIONS TO DANCE
RHYTHM

 a. "Pale Moon" .... *Logan*
 b. "To a Wild Rose" .... *McDowell*
 c. "Chansonette" .... *Friml*

GEORGE GERSHWIN (Piano)

 "A Rhapsody in Blue" .... *Gershwin*
 (*Accompanied by the Orchestra*)

IN THE FIELD OF CLASSICS

 "Pomp and Circumstance" .... *Elgar*

I was very proud of the suite the late Victor
Herbert wrote especially for that occasion. He was
a great-souled, wonderful musician and my loved
friend. His encouragement during the weeks we
were rehearsing meant a great deal to all of us. I
asked him to conduct the suite, and after he had
watched me do it, he almost consented to take my
place, because he thought I wasn't getting the most
out of his music.

"But I'll wait," he said, his eyes twinkling. "I'll
wait, Paul, until you've tried it a little longer and
then if I say to you, 'Yes, I'll be pleased to conduct
the Suite,' you'll know what I mean."

Evidently my conducting improved, for he told me at last that I did very well.

"I guess I won't take the stick, Paul," he decided. "There would always be some fool critic to say that I was better than you or you were better than me—and it might cause hard feeling."

He was joking, of course, for it would have been nearly impossible for me to have felt hard toward a genius like him and my friend as well. I relied upon his judgment always and his approval, when it came, was priceless, because it was so sincere. I am glad that he was alive to sit in a box at the first performance and bow to the cheers that greeted the playing of his Suite. Writing for a jazz orchestra was new to him and he complained a little about the doubling which he said hampered him when he wanted an oboe, say, and found the gentleman who should play the oboe busy with the bass clarinet.

"But I respected the rules of the game," he boasted, "and I might even say of this Suite, in the words of the Seventh Century nun, that even if other people do not like it, it pleases me because it is I who did it."

J a z z

"A Rhapsody in Blue" was regarded by critics as the most significant number of the program. It was the first rhapsody written for a solo instrument and a jazz orchestra. The orchestral treatment was developed by Mr. Grofe, Mr. Gershwin's manuscript being complete for the piano. It was a successful attempt to build a rhapsody out of the rhythms of popular American music. None of the thematic material had been used before. Its structure was simple and its popularity has been remarkable since we put it on the records. It is music conceived for the jazz orchestra and I do not believe any other kind of orchestra can do it full justice, though some have played it.

The audience listened attentively to everything and applauded whole-heartedly from the first moment. When they laughed and seemed pleased with "Livery Stable Blues," the crude jazz of the past, I had for a moment the panicky feeling that they hadn't realized the attempt at burlesque—that they were ignorantly applauding the thing on its merits. I experienced all sorts of qualms as the program went on, most of them unjustified, as it was.

An Experiment

A few of the men had accidents with their instruments, picking up one when they wanted another, but nobody noticed. This happens sometimes when one man plays five or six instruments. My twenty-three boys that day played thirty-six instruments.

Perhaps it would be interesting to list the instruments used in that first concert. The string section consisted of eight violins, two double basses and a banjo. There were two trumpeters, two trombonists, two pianists, a drummer, three saxophonists, and two French horn players. All these men, except the violinists and one or two others, doubled on some instrument. These extra ones included accordion, bass tuba, flugelhorns, euphonium, celesta, flute, oboe, bass oboe, heckelphone, E-flat, B-flat and bass clarinets, basset horn, Octavion, E-flat soprano, B-flat soprano, E-flat alto and E-flat baritone saxophones.

It seemed as if people would never let us go. We played all the encores we knew and still they applauded. My heart was so full I could hardly speak, as I bowed again and again. The spark that a responsive audience can always kindle in the performers had been glowing all afternoon and, as a result, we played better than I had ever hoped.

When finally we bowed for the last time, the usher brought me a pile of notes from congratulating friends and the doorman said people were waiting to see me. There was a letter from Walter Damrosch that I particularly prize. He said he thought we had done wonders with our instruments and added that he had "enjoyed every minute of it."

This friendly praise was very sweet, but I knew I must wait for the papers to learn the best or the worst. Later that week, the *Musical Digest* published a sheaf of critical comments from the dailies, and the sentiment, not merely as we culled it for publicity press notices, was divided, but on the whole encouraging.

W. J. Henderson of the *Herald* described the concert as "one of the most interesting of a busy season. Mr. Herbert's music was delightful. Mr. Gershwin's composition proved to be a highly ingenious work, treating the piano in a manner calling for much technical skill and furnishing an orchestral background in which saxophones, trombones

106

and clarinets were merged in a really skillful piece of orchestration. If this way lies the path toward the development of American modern music into a high art form, then one can heartily congratulate Mr. Gershwin on his disclosure of some of the possibilities. Nor must the captivating cleverness of Zez Confrey be forgotten. And there was Ross Gorman, a supreme virtuoso in his field, who played ten reed instruments, and Roy Maxon and Paul Whiteman himself, a born conductor and a musical personality of force and courage who is to be congratulated on his adventure and the admirable results he obtained in proving the euphony of the jazz orchestra."

"To begin with," wrote Mr. Lawrence Gilman of the *Tribune*, "Mr. Whiteman's experiment was an uproarious success. This music conspicuously possesses superb vitality and ingenuity of rhythm, mastery of novel and beautiful effects of timbre. For jazz is basically a kind of rhythm plus a kind of instrumentation. But it seems to us that this music is only half alive. Its gorgeous vitality of rhythm and of instrumental color is impaired by melodic and harmonic anemia of the most pernicious kind. Listen to the compositions of the Messrs. Archer and Kern and Gershwin.

"Ignore for a moment the fascinating rhythm and the beauty and novelty of the instrumental coloring and fasten your attention on the melodic and harmonic structure of the music. How trite and feeble and conventional the tunes are, how sentimental and vapid the harmonic treatment. Old stuff it is. Recall the most ambitious piece, the Rhapsody, and weep over the lifelessness of its melody and harmony, so derivative, so stale, so inexpressive. And then recall for contrast, the rich inventiveness of the rhythms, the saliency and vividness of the orchestral color."

Deems Taylor of the *World* found "Victor Herbert's four serenades not only charming in thematic material, but they demonstrated the fact that his skill in orchestration extends to handling the unusual instrumental combinations that a jazz band presents. George Gershwin's Rhapsody, in a way the most interesting offering, despite its shortcomings, chief of which were an occasional sacrifice of appropriate scoring to momentary effect and a lack of continuity in the musical structure—possessed at least two themes of genuine musical worth and displayed a latent ability on the part of this young composer to say something in his chosen idiom."

In the *Times*, Olin Downes mentioned "remarkably beautiful examples of scoring for a few instruments: scoring of singular economy, color and effectiveness; music at times vulgar, cheap, in poor taste, elsewhere of irresistible swing and insouciance and recklessness and life; music played as only such players as these may play it—like the melo-maniacs that they are, bitten by rhythms that would have twiddled the toes of St. Anthony.

"And then there was Mr. Whiteman. He does not conduct. He trembles, wabbles, quivers—a piece of jazz jelly, conducting the orchestra with the back of the trouser of the right leg and the face of a mandarin the while. Mr. Gershwin's composition shows extraordinary talent, just as it also shows a young composer with the aims that go far beyond those of his ilk. In spite of technical immaturity, he has expressed himself in a significant and on the whole highly original manner. This is fresh and new and full of promise."

Henry T. Finck of the *Post* thought the "Livery Stable Blues" and "Mama Loves Papa" far superior to Schoenberg, Milhaud and the rest of the "futuristic fellows. Mr. Herbert's serenades were a delightful specimen of musical mirth, melody and local color. Paul Whiteman conducted quite as well as Herbert himself could and that is the highest praise that could possibly be bestowed."

Gilbert Gabriel of the *Sun* called the concert "one long strong, musical cocktail. Whatever it was, fun or fol-de-rol, glorious, gory or just plain galumphing, it was wine that needs no bush.

"The title of the rhapsody was a just one for Mr. Gershwin's composition suitable to covering a degree of formlessness to which the middle section of the work, relying too steadily on tort and retort of the piano, seemed to lag. But the beginning and the ending of it were stunning. The beginning particularly, with a flutter-tongued, drunken whoop of an introduction that had the audience rocking. Mr. Gershwin has an irrepressible pack of talents. The Serenades were done in Mr. Herbert's ever-ready and bright style. Mr. Whiteman has some amazing musicians under him and he shines out as an extraordinarily well-rounded musician."

That was what they said. Not all compliments by any means—even in some places a suggestion of dissatisfaction with the newcomer. But after all, the critics had come to the concert instead of sending second-string men. They had devoted their lead paragraphs to it, too, and admitted its possibilities. Poor, imperfect, immature, it still was going somewhere, they said. And so the mango magic worked on.

V

What Is It?

V: What Is It?

*W*HAT is jazz?

I have been dodging this question for years, because I haven't been able to figure out an adequate answer. Probably it doesn't matter much. Whatever I think, there will be many to disagree with me. Jazz has always made a grand hostess help, for it will throw the most conservative dinner company into paroxysms of discussion and disagreement. It is a theme for which every man demands freedom of expression.

It is almost easier for a word novice like me to explain what jazz is not, than to try to say what it is. First, then, jazz is not exactly what the dictionary makes it. It has only got into the dictionary, by the way, in the last three years. The nearest to it used to be "jazey, a woolen sweater." Here is what they have inserted: "Jazz, a form of syncopated music played in discordant tone on various instruments, as the banjo, saxophone, trombone, flageolet, drum and piano."

This is obviously an uninspired, colorless way of describing a very colorful subject. Irving Berlin, who writes jazz, does better. He calls it "musical pandemonium accomplished by discords used in an ascending progression." My friend, Gilbert Seldes, writing in "Seven Lively Arts," refers to "subdominant seventh chords, successions of dominant sevenths and ninths and dissonances." Somebody, whose name has been lost to posterity unfortunately, declared illuminatingly that "Jazz is jazz and blues is blues."

I feel a good deal the same way and so does anybody who knows jazz and blues. They explain themselves, but if you don't know them, words fail to clarify them. I have heard some folks refer to jazz as an "obnoxious disease," as "musical profanity," "the true voice of the age" and the "only American art." You can readily see why I keep hedging. Who is going to find a definition to satisfy all these folks?

But to get down to business, jazz does seem to me to be, as nearly as I can express it, a musical

116

treatment consisting largely in question and answer, sound and echo. It is what I call unacademic counterpoint. It includes rhythmic, harmonic and melodic invention.

To rag a melody, one threw the rhythm out of joint making syncopation. Jazz goes further, "marking" the broken rhythm unmistakably. The great art in the jazz orchestra is a counter-balancing of the instrumentation, a realization of tone values and their placement.

With a very few but important exceptions, jazz is not as yet the thing said; it is the manner of saying it. Some critics think this fact establishes the unimportance or even the vulgarity of jazz. I believe it is true that if jazz does not develop its own theme, its own distinctive language, it will fail to be musically valuable. But it will do so.

We might, for clarity, make a rough parallel between jazz and language. In 1700, the American Colonists were beginning to speak a dialect that might be called bad English. They used tones, inflections and rhythms in words and sentences that were not the English spoken at the court of King George. They expressed themselves in that way because they were no longer living in England, they were no longer Englishmen. By their talk was revealed the change that had taken place. They said the same things that were being said on the other side of the Atlantic, but they said them differently. That is where jazz is to-day.

It was not the fact that the Colonists spoke differently that was important. The important point was that the Colonists themselves were different. The conditions in which they lived made them so. They expressed this difference first in their manner of talking. As the difference grew, they expressed it in the words they used, then in the ideas they uttered.

To-day there is an American language, a language full of new words and ideas, full of meanings that can hardly be expressed in any other tongue. A few Englishmen still speak of the American language as an "English dialect." But when they do, they simply illustrate the English slowness to admit new realities. It is—as the French say—to laugh.

We have a racy, idiomatic, flexible American language all our own, suited to expressing the American character. This, I believe, is what jazz will be—a new musical language, expressing new

meanings. Or at any rate, fresh combinations of old meanings which is all that any musical development has ever been.

To-day, however, jazz is a method of saying the old things with a twist, with a bang, with a rhythm that makes them seem new. Strictly speaking, it is instrumental effects. A large part of its technique consists of mutes being put in the brass. The first beat in any bar, which normally is accented, is passed over, and the second, third or even fourth beats are accented.

This can be roughly illustrated with a familiar bar of music. Suppose we take "Home, Sweet Home." Here it is in its original form :

Now let us jazz it up:

That won't be quite the real thing, though. The

jazz treatment is hard to put into written music. Follow the notes as carefully as you like and you will merely be like a person trying to imitate, for instance, a Southern accent—unless jazz is in your blood. If it is, you'll add the indefinable thing to the notes—that spontaneous jazzing—that will make the music talk jazz as a native tongue.

While we are still using the old themes in this way, it isn't every composition that will lend itself to jazz treatment. This is because music is not only a succession of sounds. It is also quality of sound. It is really not very satisfactory to take anything written for a symphony and try to play it with a jazz orchestra. That is the same, in principle, as taking a composition scored for an orchestra and trying to play it on the piano. And how would Debussy's "L'Aprés Midi d'un Faune" sound on an organ? Imagine trying to get the tone and color of that lovely composition in any such way.

I suppose it will surprise a good many people to have me say that some things can't be jazzed. And as a matter of fact, it is not literally true. Almost anything can be played by a jazz group on jazz instruments in the jazz manner. Anything can be jazzed—that is, subjected to jazz treatment.

But it is not fitting to jazz everything. And common sense, together with a loving knowledge of music, will indicate whether to jazz or not. I might mention for instance "Onward, Christian Soldiers," which should not be jazzed. There is a sturdy, majestic tune with a religious connotation. We could jazz it easily, but we wouldn't. Neither would we jazz the "Tannhäuser" march nor any of the lovely operatic arias. On the other hand, there would be no sacrilege in jazzing "Dixie," even though the tune is deep in the hearts of a Southern people. And "Song of India," which we did jazz, was a ballet in the first place, so that was all right. It is just a matter of feeling. Some things were written for sober, sublime moments. They should be left for such moments. They do not fit jazz. But the "Peer Gynt" suite, the "Poet and Peasant" overture—why not jazz them?

Jazz then is a method. But it's not only a method of counterpoint and rhythm; it's also a method of using tones, using the color of sound. The instruments for making jazz music are, as I shall point out, legitimate and have been used in

121

various combinations for making serious music.

I have already spoken of the original meaning of the word jazz. John Philip Sousa, who with his military band, by the way, has come nearer the hearts of the people than any musical institution America ever has had, says jazz slid into our vocabulary by way of the vaudeville stage, where at the end of a performance, all the acts came back on the stage to give a rousing, boisterous *finale* called a "jazzbo." There is also a legend that a particularly jazzy darky player, named James Brown and called "Jas" from the abbreviation of his name, was the source of the peppy little word that has now gone all over the world.

At any rate, in spite of its early troubles, many are now anxious to claim the word, and to my mind, New Orleans presents perhaps the best evidence. Maybe some future encyclopedia will settle the moot question for us. The compilers will have to build the case on a good deal of supposition, but once we see it all written down without any "I suppose's" and "probably's," we shall be set at ease.

Also, some future chronicler will undoubtedly answer another popular query: "Is it art?"

VI

Is It Art?

VI: Is It Art?

I DON'T really care whether jazz is art or not. There is always a hubbub going on about art and I can't see that it gets anywhere. A good part of the controversy depends upon definition and I would rather be working to do something than to define it, any day.

Webster says art is "a system of rules or of organized modes of operation serving to facilitate the performance of certain actions—an occupation having to do with the theory or practice of taste in the expression of beauty in form, color, sound, speech or movement."

That is too complicated for me. I think art is merely the capturing in some form of a bit of universal beauty. Still, let Mr. Webster and any other man have his opinion just so long as he doesn't make art out to be snobbishness. Snobbish worries about art have never done much but annoy and hinder the real artist.

Jazz

It is fairly safe to say that those folks who scorn everything American because being American, it can't be artistic, and despise everything the common people like, would have been a good deal the same in Athens when the Acropolis was being built. As sure as fate, they'd have been mourning for the pure art of ancient Crete and talking about the vulgar commercialism of Greece. It's a way we mortals have.

The Greek sculptors and musicians and dramatists weren't talking much about art. They were too busy working. There was the same difference between the talkers and the artists that there is to-day.

To me the test of art is its appeal to great masses of humanity. The artist must say something that is intelligible to all the people. He must go so deep that he touches the basic human. He always has, if he has been real. It was the people of Athens who cheered Praxiteles, and the Florentines, the crowds in the street, whose verdict settled the fate of the works of Andrea del Sarto and Leonardo da Vinci.

In music, the same thing has happened. All the masters have suffered heartbreak and discouragement because the cultured few whose judgment was taken as a criterion refused to countenance anything new. It was the common people who found beauty in the fresh forms and insisted upon a hearing for the artists.

I hope I have not seemed to say that everything that is popular is art. I claim no artistic distinction for the teddy bear or the cross word puzzle. But I do believe that the so-called art which is reserved for the art-snobbish few goes as far from the line in one direction as the teddy bear does in the other.

Beauty is emotion, not intellect—and emotion is universal. Nobody needs a long course of schooling in order to respond to beauty. The first response is instinctive, fundamental, out of the depths of human emotion. And it is only when a work appeals to the depths of human emotion that it has any chance to outlive its generation.

Beauty is sometimes found in unbeautiful subjects. It is the treatment that counts, not the theme. If the design is to shock, then that is bad art. Sometimes jazz deals with unbeautiful themes, but the best of it is trying to make something beautiful out of its material.

Music has never had a chance to reach the multitudes in America. Yet they respond to it whenever they have the opportunity. The masses of the people of America are fundamentally the same in artistic appreciation, or the lack of it, as the masses of the people of Europe. Americans are, after all, the same blood, with the same age-old cultural background. And good music is sung and hummed and whistled from Moscow to Naples, from Cherbourg to Budapest.

As far as the matter of appreciation is concerned, there is no earthly reason why the classics should not be the daily musical preoccupation of working men, stock brokers and farmers from New York to San Francisco. They never have been because there has always been this rigid wall of insulation, put up by the highbrows.

Highbrowism was slipped over on us. Our pioneer grandfathers were too busy keeping alive in the wilderness to spend any time learning to be "cultured." The backwoodsmen, the Indian fighters, the farmers on the frontier were cut off from all music except a few simple melodies—old English folk songs and American songs of the same type. This is very lovely music, but our forefathers didn't think of it as music because a few rich folks in the cities had a copyright on the word. They aped everything European and imported music with their fashions and their books.

The first attempt to popularize music was the humble beginning of Tin Pan Alley, New York's great street of popular song. A corset salesman who loved music was among the first of the melody manufacturers. The early efforts were in the main tawdry and banal. Perhaps you remember "Smoky Mokes," "A Hot Time in the Old Town," "The Curse of An Aching Heart."

Even then the pieces that really took hold on the popular fancy had some flavor of real music. Mendelssohn's "Spring Song" had a mighty fascination for the man in the street and everybody sang the melody in popular songs thinly disguised.

The beauty of the original theme caught the ear, but the crudity of the development proved tiresome, so that the fashion in songs shifted constantly. The public felt the same uneasy dissatisfaction that

it feels with style in clothes, which not being basically beautiful, is constantly changed for something new. At the same time, this banality was
spoiling the ear and debauching the taste.

Then the phonograph companies came along and
began to put out good records. It is to the credit
of the American people that there was a general
response, and instantaneous, to this new musical
opportunity. But nothing in music really took hold
of the whole population until jazz set all America
humming, singing, dancing.

Jazz is not in the "tradition" of music, according to the old sense, but is not the real tradition
of music one of constant change and new develop-
ments? Jazz is the spirit of a new country. It
catches up the underlying life motif of a continent
and period, molding it into a form which expresses
the fundamental emotion of the people, the place
and time so authentically that it is immediately
recognizable.

At the same time, it evolves new forms, new
colors, new technical methods, just as America constantly throws aside old machines for newer and
more efficient ones.

Is It Art?

I think it is a mistake to call jazz cheerful. The optimism of jazz is the optimism of the pessimist who says, "Let us eat, drink and be merry, for tomorrow we die."

This cheerfulness of despair is deep in America. Our country is not the childishly jubilant nation that some people like to think it. Behind the rush of achievement is a restlessness of dissatisfaction, a vague nostalgia and yearning for something indefinable, beyond our grasp.

A few discerning critics have heard this in jazz —but they call it a hint of the Russian, or a flavor of the Oriental. That is because, for some unknown reason, writers and critics generally talk of the "soul of Russia" and the "soul of the Orient." Apparently nobody ever thinks of crediting America with a soul.

We are supposed to be a nation of crass materialists. We are supposed to care for nothing but money. We care probably less for material things, less for money than any people on earth.

We want something—something beautiful, good, satisfying; and with our tremendous energy we keep building and destroying and building again, in our passionate desire to have it—a desire never satisfied. That is the thing expressed by that wail, that longing, that pain, behind all the surface clamor and rhythm and energy of jazz. The critics may call it Oriental, call it Russian, call it anything they like. It is an expression of the soul of America and America recognizes it.

Some months ago, Simeon Strunsky, writing in the New York *Times*, rebuked the flood of writers who constantly speak of jazz as the expression of the American spirit.

"Does it," asked Mr. Strunsky, "express President Coolidge, our party system, our Rotary club, our Puritanism, our capitalism and our Ku Klux Klan?"

No, jazz does not represent these varying aspects of America, any more than it represents hot cakes, corn on the cob, grapefruit and meat for breakfast. What it does represent is the indefinable thing which will mark the Puritan President Coolidge, the Irish Tammany ward leader, Harry Sinclair, Babbitt and Mr. Simeon Strunsky himself, every one of them, as Americans, in any city of

Europe. It represents the composite essence of them all.

That essence, if I may be forgiven for taking the liberty of attempting to describe anything so elusive, is energetic, wistful, enterprising and self-confident, above a substratum of humility.

Of course, anybody else who likes may take a fling at defining Americanism and do it better than I. But whether we can say what it means or not, Americanism is recognized by us all, and not only by us, but by every foreign shopkeeper who sees it coming from afar.

As to whether jazz is or is not art—does it matter what we label it, if it lives and brings new beauty into life? And if it does not—then the label matters even less.

VII

Jazz in America

VII: Jazz in America

THE jazz age has been the subject of profound and careful condemnation. I found, when I went to put together these notes, that while comparatively little has been written in an analytical way about jazz, as music, the criticisms, constructive and otherwise, of so-called jazz manners and morals, would fill a library.

I have kept a jazz clipping file for nearly five years and whenever I feel blue, I take it out. It is more enlivening than a vaudeville show. Ministers, club women, teachers and parents have been seeing in jazz a menace to the youth of the nation ever since the word came into general use. They have claimed that it put the "sin" in "syncopation." They have scolded at it, satirized it, "suppressed" it. Nothing has done any good.

"Jazz music causes drunkenness," one despatch quotes Dr. E. Elliott Rawlings of New York as saying. "The quick and staccato tempo of jazz music, with the plaintive and pleading notes of the violin and the clarinet, the imploring tones of the saxophone, the rhythmic beating of the drums—all these send a continuous whirl of impressionable stimulations to the brain, producing thoughts and imaginations which overpower the will. Reason and reflection are lost and the actions of the person are directed by the stronger animal passions. In other words, jazz affects the brain through the sense of hearing, giving the same results as whisky or any other alcoholic drinks taken into the system by way of the stomach. It has the same effect as a drug and one may become addicted to its use."

Wails the president of the Christian and Missionary Alliance Conference: "American girls of tender age are approaching jungle standards . . . little American girls are maturing too quickly under the hectic influence of jazz and speed."

The next generation, this same missionary goes on to relate, will see women old in their twenties, unless the jazz tendency is halted. The jazz spirit of the times was blamed by Dr. Harry M. Warren, president of the Save-a-Life League, in his 1924 report, for many of the fifteen thousand suicides in the United States.

Nathan Ketelovitch, a musician, was said to have been driven mad by his hatred for jazz music. He came from Missouri.

"The jazz band view of life is wrecking the American home," declared Professor Herman Derry, speaking in Detroit, Michigan.

Dr. Florence H. Richards, medical director of the William Penn High School for Girls, Philadelphia, based her opposition to jazz on a long and careful study of the reactions of 3,800 girls to that kind of music.

"The objection of the physician," she explains, "is the effect that jazz has on certain human emotions. All sorts of excuses may be made for it, but the consensus of opinion of leading medical and other scientific authorities is that its influence is as harmful and degrading to civilized races as it always has been among the savages from whom we borrowed it. If we permit our boys and girls to be exposed indefinitely to this pernicious influence, the harm that will result may tear to pieces our whole social fabric."

More than one American city, instituting music week, has become divided in its citizenry over the question of whether jazz shall or shall not be played —in short, whether jazz is or is not, music.

A famous domestic economist rose recently to remark that jazz is cheating the home since folks are spending on dances and cafés the money they might otherwise put into wall paper and saucepans.

A Canadian physician produced statistics to show that jazz had doubled insanity in the United States. I sometimes think there are statistics to prove anything.

A specialist in diseases of the ear and throat declared that if the epidemic of "bees knees," "Apple Sauces" and "Dadas" continued, a whole nation would be overwhelmed with ear paralysis.

Because her husband was so fond of the great American noise that he played "What'll I Do" on the victrola until 4 A.M. six days a week, an Ohio wife was granted a divorce. Just about the same time, Judge Lamberton of Illinois said that three-fourths of the divorces in his court were caused by jazz.

An Arkansas man bought up an entire pleasure resort so that he could ban jazz in the place. Thomas Edison was quoted as saying that he usually played jazz records backwards because they sounded better that way. A poet complained that jazz was drowning the music of the spheres— that the man who wants to commune with the stars finds his efforts balked by radio. (Personally, I never heard a radio in any dewy lane. But then I'm not a poet.)

A committee on "Sabbath and Family Religion" found, after careful deliberation, the morale of the average American family in a state of terrible jazz.

Writing in a contest on the value of music in the home, a Japanese new to this country put in a word against the prisoner at the bar when he said: "Music for use in the home must have natural sound. If we seek a better home by means of music, we may find it, except by jazz, which is not in nature."

In a small Nebraska town, jazz was classed as a public nuisance. Not far away in Kansas, a determined historian found in jazz a new cause for the fall of the Roman Empire. (My own idea would be that Rome fell because the Romans had to read Cæsar. In the days when I had to do that, I would have been equal to razing any town.)

I do not want to seem continually to be defending jazz. I am too conscious of its faults and its crudities to be its gallant knight, anyway. But I really do think, in spite of all the talk, that the effect of jazz on American morals is just nothing at all.

If flappers flap and jazz jazzes, neither one is the effect of the other. They are both effects of the fundamental character of the times. It used to be the fad to blame the War for everything the moralists didn't like. Now one berates jazz— that's all. Besides an attack on jazz has a lot of publicity value.

As a matter of fact, the War merely accelerated the speed of the movement that was under way in 1913, and jazz merely expresses it. It will take a hundred years or more to get a perspective on what's the matter, if anything. It took a hundred years to find out what was the matter with life in the early nineteenth century and Europe was then having almost the same kind of turmoil we are having now, due to the revolutions and wars of the late eighteenth century.

Everybody thought the world was going to the dogs. There were crime waves and suicide epidemics. The Greenwich Villagers and Bohemians of the time advocated excesses that are unprintable now, wild as we are supposed to be. Yet the world didn't go to the dogs and the chances are that it won't this time.

Certainly, if it does, I for one, shall never hold jazz responsible. As a matter of fact, why isn't it a good deal better to express one's self in song rather than in action? Making unholy yowls with a saxophone, or even dancing till breakfast time in a state of exuberant, joyous excitement doesn't usually have any effect more serious than sending the jazzer to sleep completely tired out.

Not long ago in the clinical notes of the *American Mercury*, I found some interesting paragraphs on music and sin.

"Jazz," wrote Mr. Mencken or Mr. Nathan, "is not voluptuous at all. Its monotonous rhythms

143

and puerile tunes make it a sedative rather than a stimulant. Jazz, which came in with prohibition, gets the blame which belongs to its partner. In the old days when it was uncommon for refined women to get drunk at dances, it would have been quite harmless. To-day, even Chopin's Funeral March would be dangerous."

Then the writer goes on to recall James Huneker's story of the prudent opera mama who refused to let her daughter sing "Isolde" on the ground that no woman could ever get through the second act without forgetting God—and adds that there are piano pieces of Chopin, not to mention Puccini's "La Boheme," that are a hundred times worse than "Isolde." The "Salome" and "Elektra" of Richard Strauss have been prohibited by the police, at one time or another, in nearly every country of the world—and these instances could be multiplied.

Almost everybody has some theory of what's wrong with the world. Those who don't blame jazz because it expresses too much, are blaming the lingering traces of Puritanism because it represses too much. I firmly believe the world will wag along about as usual, regardless of fanatics and crusaders and all their theories. If I thought jazz was actually doing any harm, I should worry most sincerely. The charge of wrecking the home life, menacing the youth and throwing an entire nation into criminal ways is not a pleasant one at any odds, even if one is only supposed to have helped in the disastrous campaign.

But when the evidence is all in, I think we can refute the charge. When you eliminate from the mass of attacks on jazz all those that obviously came out of some one's desire for notoriety and all the others—like the divorce cases—that were written because some newspaper reporter wanted to jazz up a dull story, there remains, it seems to me, only one serious ground for objecting to jazz. That is the effect the rhythms have on the emotions—their intoxicating effect.

There's no question whatever about it. Jazz does stir up the whole human being. I believe that some scientific experiments have been made which show that listening to jazz increases the heart-beat, raises the temperature, quickens the respiration, and makes all the senses more acute. It is quite true that people get drunk on jazz. Nor is it old

145

wine to sip. Rather it is a valiant, strident Martini to gulp, warming the blood at once and quickening the senses.

But it is yet to be proved that getting drunk on jazz does anybody any harm. My own opinion is that it does everyone good. I'm heartily in favor of that kind of intoxication.

There's no getting away from the fact that human beings—and all the animals, too—will get drunk. It seems as though life needs intoxication now and then. Needs to be stirred up, quickened, made breathless and excited. Cats go miles to find catnip and get drunk on it. Mice get together in great crowds and run in circles until they're so dizzy they can't stand up. Elephants in the jungles will assemble every so often and mill around until they work themselves into a kind of frenzy. And every society of human beings known upon this earth has had intoxicants—not only drinks and drugs of various kinds, but seasons of intoxicating themselves with song and dance. The lowest sub-men in the jungles of Africa have these seasons in common with the ancient Greeks, citizens of the highest civilization in the modern world. That is to say, both the savages and Greeks get drunk on song and dance.

More than that, every human being has some kind of intoxication. I know there are lots of worthy men and women who won't believe this for a minute. Tell them they get drunk and they'll be horrified. They'll assure you they have never tasted a drop of intoxicating liquor in their lives and never expect to. There's nothing they hate more than Demon Rum.

I don't doubt it. But they're missing the fact that getting drunk doesn't necessarily have anything whatever to do with drinking.

Depend upon it, when you really know them, you will find they all have some way of intoxicating themselves—some way of stirring up their emotions, getting excited, living more vividly than normally. I never knew it to fail. Sometimes they get drunk on poetry, sometimes on religion, sometimes they get their release, their frenzy, in the very fury with which they attack drink—as Carrie Nation did. Sometimes they are militant suffragists, or work-till-they-drop settlement teachers.

Whatever they are, every human being, from

the highest to the lowest, from the pulpit to the gutter, wants this sense of fuller life, this intoxication of body and spirit. And every human being gets it—somehow, sometime.

Now of course, there are scores, maybe hundreds of ways of getting this intoxication. Some are good and some are bad. Maybe my use of the word intoxication in this sense, applying it to the good intoxications as well as to the bad, may offend some good people. I hope not. My dictionary says that the word "intoxicate" means to excite to enthusiasm or madness.

In this sense, then, the ecstasies of the saint, the fervor of reformers and social workers, the spiritual experiences that take a human being temporarily away from the humdrum things of this world, are all intoxications. The other end of the scale is the stupor of the drug addict who lies in the gutter dead to the world, but intensely living in some gorgeous dream.

Jazz as an intoxicant comes somewhere between these two extremes, obviously. My own notion is that it is well on the upper side of the line that divides good from bad. I firmly believe that jazz, as an intoxicant, is a tremendous influence for good in the world.

The super-intoxicant works through rhythm. Now, I don't know a thing about the fundamental meanings of rhythm, and I doubt if anybody does. All I have been able to find written on the subject seems to me to be merely words—a sort of game of chasing definitions. But I do know that rhythm is somehow bound up with the very deepest centers of life. There's rhythm in everything—in the seasons, in the courses of the stars, in the beating of the heart, the rise and fall of the diaphragm, in day and night, waking and sleeping, birth and death.

Maybe this will seem fantastic, but I almost believe that everything wrong—disease of the body, unhappiness in the spirit—may be due to a disturbance of the natural rhythms. Maybe these intoxications that every living thing needs and gets somehow are simply a shaking-back into the right rhythms.

Could it be that the difference between the good intoxications and the bad is simply this: that the good intoxications get one back into the right rhythms—"in tune with the infinite," as the New Thought people call it—and that the bad intoxications do the same thing temporarily but leave one more out of tune than before. As, of course, drink and drugs do.

All this is rather highbrow stuff for a plain ordinary man like me who doesn't know anything but music and not much about that. But these are my ideas and when we come right down to earth, most people can check up on them from their own experiences. There's hardly a person living who hasn't known what it was to be blue and out of sorts and cheered just at the worst moment by a lively bit of rhythm.

Street crowds are constantly being dragged out of collective gloom by barrel organs, or outdoor phonographs or passing bands. Try some time standing across the street from one of those wheezy, asthmatic mechanical pianos that play in front of neighborhood motion picture theaters. Hundreds of people pass by, absorbed in their own affairs, looking tired and dispirited. (And it's astonishing when you see the faces of crowds, how few of them look as if they ever had worn a smile.) But as

Jazzing the Florida Boom at Coral Gables

soon as they come within sound of the rhythm, they begin to seem more lively. Their heads come up, their feet go more briskly, keeping time, time, time. Their eyes brighten and their whole aspect changes. It is almost as if they had penetrated into another world.

And this effect will last for two or three blocks beyond the sound of the music. Then the crowd becomes dull again. But it becomes no duller than before. There is no reaction, no katzenjammer after being cheered up by rhythms.

I firmly believe jazz has the power to take people out of a dull world, to shake them up, to give them an intoxication of rhythm and movement which makes them happy, makes them better, makes them live more intensely. Even the nostalgia, lament and longing that are in jazz create a form of happiness because they express something that lies deep in the soul.

I believe the ill effects of jazz which are so widely advertised come not from jazz at all but from other things that are sometimes combined with jazz. I don't say that a person who spends all night in a stuffy, hot, smoke-filled room, probably drinking bad liquor, won't wake up in the morning with a headache. He—or she—will be lucky if the headache is the extent of the damage. The fact that a man has been dancing to the rhythms of a jazz orchestra isn't going to save him from nicotine poisoning or from going crazy on wood alcohol.

Jazz itself is good for what ails most people, but it isn't a cure-all or patent nostrum. When I hear people blaming it for all the crime, all the suicides, all the wrecks of young girlhood—as though these things had never been heard of before jazz was invented, I am reminded of a story I once heard about vaccination.

"I don't believe in vaccination," said the farmer, "my neighbor's little boy was vaccinated in school and within a week, he was dead. None of my children will ever be vaccinated—not if I know it."

"Did the little boy die of the vaccination or of small-pox?" somebody asked.

"Neither. He fell out of a tree and broke his neck."

People forget that jazz to-day is a national music—a part of the whole American life which includes housewives, business men, boys and girls

—and not by any means confined to the occasional low dance hall. And they blame it for all the harm that evil influences do. They might as reasonably give it credit for all the good that good influences accomplish.

I don't go to the extreme of the latter. But I do believe—and here of course and perhaps not for the first time in the course of this book—I shall be accused of rank over-partiality; though I am only giving my honest and thoughtful opinion—that spiritually jazz is saving America from calamity.

Professor Patterson of Columbia University says somewhere in his studies of rhythm that the music of contemporary savages taunts us with a lost art. Modern life, he points out, has inhibited many normal instincts, and the mere fact that our conventional dignity forbids us to sway our bodies, to tap our feet when we hear rhythmic music, has deprived us of normal outlets for natural impulses.

I will go even farther than that. I believe all the tendencies of modern living—of machine civilization—are to make crippled, perverted things of human beings. The machines are standardizing everything. There never was before such an era

153

of standardization as there is to-day in the United States. It invades everything, crushing all the normal impulses of human beings.

At their work, men and women are the victims of efficiency, the Taylor system, so that humanity itself is being made into machines. On their way home, on the streets, in the cars, subways, trains, humans are transported in masses, like wheat run through a mill. The tremendous business machines, turning out millions of standard products, dress us all alike, feed us alike, give us the same things to read, the same ideas, the same outlook on life, the same manners, the same slang.

There is increasingly less room for individuality and humanity revolts against this pressure. Human energies have got to break through it somewhere. Human beings aren't machines. They aren't standardized products, all alike. They can't stand living in masses, under compulsion; working all at the same speed in the same kind of offices, in the same kind of factories, at the same kind of machines; playing in masses, all packed in the same grandstands, watching the same professionals play the same games.

Human beings want to run, to dance, to sing. They want to play and to express themselves in their play. They've got to do it, or all that dammed-up energy is going to break loose in something a lot worse than play. The Machine Age is as bad as the Puritan Age, in that it brings repression.

In America, jazz is at once a revolt and a release. Through it, we get back to a simple, to a savage, if you like, joy in being alive. While we are dancing or singing or even listening to jazz, all the artificial restraints are gone. We are rhythmic, we are emotional, we are natural. We're really living—living to a pitch that becomes an intoxication. And it's good living. The world seems brighter, troubles don't weigh so heavily, the natural joy and delight there is in just being alive comes to the surface. That is a good experience. After it, one goes back to everyday affairs rid of the pressure of the suppressed play spirit, refreshed and ready for work and difficulties.

This, it seems to me, is the great value of jazz in American life.

Jazz has affected America, however, in a musical way, and in many more material senses. It is bulking increasingly large in economics. There are to-day more than 200,000 men playing it. The number of jazz arrangers is around 30,000. Thus two entirely new industries have grown up in less than ten years.

They are lucrative industries, too. Players in the best of the modern jazz orchestras have come straight from the symphonies where they were paid $30, $40, or at the most $50 and $60 a week. Now they get $150 up.

Jazz has made fortunes and bought automobiles, country houses and fur coats for many a player, composer and publisher. Indirectly it has filled the pockets of the musicians who are identified with opera and symphony, for it has interested a greater part of the population in music.

The accessories of jazz figure conspicuously in the buying and selling of the nation. In 1924, the United States spent $600,000,000 for music and musical instruments, and Tin Pan Alley claims that eighty per cent. of that amount, or $480,000,000, was paid out for jazz and jazz-making instruments.

It cost ninety per cent. of the rest of the world approximately the same sum to get completely jazzed up. The foreign market for American music in pre-jazz times was poor. Tin Pan Alley not only had no special selling facilities abroad, but also Europe wrote most of the world's popular song hits and America bought them—songs like "Rings on My Fingers" and "Has Anybody Here Seen Kelly?"

Then jazz of the irresistible appeal came along and the whole situation was reversed. A representative of the largest music publishing firm in London, with branches all over the continent, said in New York the other day that jazz has shot the formerly stable English ballad market all to pieces. Nobody wants to sing old-fashioned sentiment any more. And so jazz takes its place among profitable American exports.

It is a striking commentary on the possibilities of jazz-making that so many young college graduates are going straight from the classroom to the jazz orchestra. I do not know the exact figures, because as yet the colleges are a little embarrassed about the jazz players they turn out. I know unofficially, however, of one school that has fifteen future jazzists among its hundred seniors. Another class of two hundred has twenty-five prospective jazz leaders and ten men out of two hundred and ten in a third school have announced that they hope to join the liveliest art of all.

Musically as I have tried to show, jazz has helped thousands to a glimpse of the beauty of the classics. I believe this country will want to see more of the classics, but the people will never forget jazz, whether it ever gets to be an art or not.

Another thing jazz has done is to develop the finest set of brass players the country has even known. This is admitted even by musicians who are otherwise prejudiced against the great American noise.

Jazz has fostered originality among players and has aroused a whole nation to an interest in music, opening our eyes and ears wider to the message of new writers. It is waking the people of America to a spontaneous interest in all kinds of music, giving all musicians a larger native audience. Not because of jazz, but through it, we are becoming musically a self-confident people. Won't that help?

VIII

Tin Pan Alley

VIII: Tin Pan Alley

*T*IN PAN ALLEY was the grade school of jazz. Nowadays, the little pupil with the tin dinner pail has passed on to institutions of higher learning. But for all that, Tin Pan Alley still claims her and in the main, acts as her guardian and caretaker.

Perhaps the Alley has caught a little of the spirit of uplift, too. At any rate, not so long ago, prominent song writers sent up an official plaint for a new name for their stamping ground. They wanted, they said, a name that would be more dignified and express, to some extent, the true ideals and aspirations of the famous old street.

Like everybody else, I think of the Alley as a street. As a matter of fact, Tin Pan Alley exists now only as a tradition. The original alley was on West 28th Street between Fifth and Sixth Avenues, New York. I am told that it was in 1899 that the publishing firm of Witmark & Sons moved "way up town" to 51 West 28th Street, the wholesale florist section, from 13th and Broadway. Then, Broder & Schlam, publishers from San Francisco, also moved over and were followed in due time by Chas. K. Harris, Leo Feist and others.

Thus Tin Pan Alley was born and though the christening was delayed for a while, it came off in due season under the auspices, I believe, of a newspaper man who had taken up song writing.

In late years, Tin Pan Alley has scattered. Music publishers ply their trade all along the Forties on both sides of Broadway. I do not think, however, that it is the inaccuracy that troubles song writers about the name. It is only that—well, you can see for yourself that Tin Pan Alley has certain intimations of informality not suitable for higher art.

Just the same, the name will stick and I am glad. There is a deal of poetry and memory in the phrase that for more than twenty-five years has served a useful purpose. Why should it be turned off now, like an old servant who has outgrown his place?

The Alley is one of my favorite haunts. I can

well understand that the clatter of hundreds of
pianos above which rise hundreds of voices trying
out new songs is Bedlam to the stranger. To me,
however, and to all the other habitués of the place
these are only the signs of a thriving market. For
perish the day when the pianos are stilled and the
voices otherwise employed! This will mean that
some new-fangled mode of entertainment has been
discovered by those who please the fickle public.
For the present, Tin Pan Alley is the commissary
for America's 8,000,000 phonographs, her 9,000,-
000 hand-played and 800,000 foot-played pianos.

But never let anybody tell you that the Alley is
not business-like. There are as many yards of red
tape wound about the "Mammy" song that finally
reaches you as there are about the automobile produced in any up-to-date factory. Tin Pan Alley is
divided into departments with heads, super and
under, clerks, secretaries, telephone operators and
authors. It takes as many long-drawn-out confer-
ences, house messages on blue, yellow, pink and
green sheets of paper to run a song factory as it
does to build a skyscraper. For the Tin Pan Alley
factory generally takes its product straight through

from the first step to the last. The first step is composition. There is, of course, a chance that you may write a song which will earn you $25,000, as George Cohan's "Over There" did for him, but that chance is exceedingly thin. Do they look at your manuscript? Yes, usually. That is, if you have consigned it with special tenderness to their care, writing in ink, or even better, on the typewriter and on one side of the paper. Also, it is well to send your offering registered. An official of one of the largest publishing houses admits that a song manuscript which comes into his office unregistered is returned to the sender without an examination.

"I figure," says the publisher, "that if the writer puts no very high value on his product, I shall not be able to. Besides, the registered ones keep a large office force hard at work. And we don't get much out of it. I can count on the fingers of one hand the hits that we have been able to draw from the millions of contributions that come in."

He can give no adequate reason for the outlander not being able to write acceptable songs. Perhaps it is because the popular song phrasing changes almost in a minute. What is hot slang one week has become stale and almost forgotten by the next.

Still there are occasionally some strange freaks. Leo Wood, who has made several home runs off his hits in times past, collected on one that was ten years old.

In 1914, this composer wrote a song called "Somebody Stole My Gal." The song was a flop, in the technical language of the Alley—that is, it did not sell. It was shelved and Wood forgot about it, as experimenters in the Alley are likely to do, having learned that even the smartest of them will never be able to work out the exact formula for a hit. Ten years later, a pal around the shop called, "Hey, Wood, congratulations on your new hit!"

"What d'ye mean?" asked Wood.

"Why, your hit—'Somebody Stole **My Gal**.' Didn't you know you had a hit?"

All excited, Wood began to investigate and found that sure enough his ancient and completely unsung effort was now selling like the proverbial hot cakes. At first, he was completely puzzled. Then he found out that the song was being plugged by former students of the University of Pennsylvania who had liked it and played it in their school orchestra when it was first brought out. One of the men became an orchestra leader and others were interested in professional or amateur musical organizations throughout the United States. They played "Somebody Stole My Gal" until they made a hit of it.

"That's What God Made Mothers For" also got to be a hit ten years after it was written. In the interim, it gained popularity in England and was brought back to New York as a song suitable for Mothers' Day. Now it makes a lot of money for its publisher and author.

George Cohan has a little song in which he tells you exactly how to compose a popular hit. First, you make up a little rhyme and then put it to music on the piano. After that, you take it to the publisher and he puts it in all the shop windows for everybody to buy. Naturally, then, you have, says George, a hit. Just as easy, he adds, as falling off a log. It does sound simple, doesn't it? And he makes it work.

Most popular music is written on assignment.

That is, the head of the sales department, the professional manager, or one of the arrangers decides that it is time to have a certain kind of song. He takes the matter up with the proper heads of departments and if everybody agrees, the particular tunesmith who specializes in that variety of work is told to get busy. The staff usually contains experts in mammy, mama, and mother songs, if you get the distinction. And that is another reason why the outsider fails to land. He doesn't know about these vogues. This is, as has frequently been said, an age of specialization.

I am told that generally the professional manager, the head of the sales department and one of the arrangers, form a jury to accept or reject songs. They get more practice in rejecting than accepting. But when occasionally they accept and the lyrics have been fitted with music, or the tune with lyrics as the case may happen to be, the real work of putting out a popular song begins.

The first step is engraving the plates by hand. This is delicate work. It is said there are only fifty men in the country capable of doing it. Just imagine what the effect would be if the stem of a note were to be broken off or if a half note were to be filled in by accident, making it appear to be a quarter. That is why sheet music is not printed but lithographed. Millions of copies can be run off in this way and often millions are. The first of these are the copyright copies which must be forwarded to the Library of Congress. Professional copies, prepared for the artists who will plug the songs, come next. Then there are vocal orchestrations prepared in several different keys. Small motion picture theaters throughout the country use art slides with the chorus surrounded by a flary border to be flashed on the screen after the soloist has sung the verse and the audience is being besought to join in on the chorus.

In this day of many orchestras, the orchestrations for bands, jazz and non-jazz are almost as important as the song plugger himself. And the song plugger has always been the chief voice of the Alley. It is his job to sing loudly and convincingly into whatever ears he can reach. He goes everywhere he can break in—to motion picture houses, benefits, picnics, races, circuses and social gatherings. He really needs to be an adventurous soul and one who takes rebuffs lightly. Every day in a New York vaudeville theater, two song pluggers climb up several hundred feet among the pipes of an organ and sing almost from the ceiling to a puzzled audience who try to figure where the music is coming from.

While plugging is important, the publishers contended recently that there can be too much of any good thing. The "too much" in this case was radio. So the publishers and composers sued the radio people to compel them to pay a royalty every time a popular song is sung over the radio. Their argument was that if John Smith tunes in every night on a red hot mama song, he may soon begin to wish never to hear that particular song again. And this, say the publishers and composers, will undoubtedly hurt the sale of the piece of sheet music.

The type of plugging which takes a song all over the country is done by the various vocal artists. These men and women get their songs from the professional offices, and comedians like Al Jolson and Fanny Brice can "make" almost any number. Nearly always after a number is sensationally popular, a story gets out about starving youths who have sold their inspiration for the price of a meal and continued to starve while the publisher deposits new millions from its sale and fails even to send flowers when the defrauded youths at last expire of malnutrition. I suppose there have been instances almost as sad as this, but what with the sophistication gained from the movies, which reveals practically everybody as a potential villain and the radio, which broadcasts not only news about profitable investments but also the etiquette for any occasion, I doubt if there are many dupes left in the world. Most of those who write popular songs demand an advance of something like a thousand dollars. The usual author's royalty on the song is about two cents on each copy of sheet music. The mechanical royalties arising from phonograph and piano roll records are usually protected in the contract.

One of the most pathetic figures along Broadway is the "one-song man." He is the person who has created a single hit and has never been able to pull it off again but neglects everything else in the vain hope that some day he may repeat. You will find his type in almost every line of creative work. I know one man who wrote a short story that won two prizes and the praise of Rudyard Kipling. That man is now an embittered, discouraged farmer in the Middle West. He is a one-story man.

Sometimes, song writers bob up in strange places. Phil Kornheiser, genius hit-picker for the flourishing Feist Publishing concern, was astonished one day to get a manuscript from his chauffeur and to find, moreover, that it was good. Elevator boys, truck drivers, and society buds are others who have sprung surprises on him from time to time.

Jazz, the latest phase of American popular music, is the hardest of all to write, the tunesmiths say. The lyrics, however, are easier. Previous to 1897 every song had to have six or seven verses and each verse had eight or ten lines. Now there are two verses of a scant four lines each, and even at that, the second verse counts scarcely at all. The whole story must be told in the first verse and chorus and usually there is very little to it anyway, the music being what matters.

In the old days, it took six months to spread even the most sure-fire song over the United States, for there was no radio and the orchestras were few and far between. To-day, the provinces beat New York to almost everything. Not many of the old-time song writers, the men who produced the ballads and coon songs of another era, have been able to break themselves in to the new vogue. They are too verbose.

Somebody recently lent me an old volume of pre-Tin Pan Alley songs, some dating as far back as 1835.

Among the ballad writers of the Forties was Dr. J. K. Mitchell, the plot of whose "I've Waited Long" was, he said, taken from life.

"In composing a song," he explained in a fore-word to his publishers, "I always fall into a strain, which, according to accident, is original or recollected. The one I now send you is a simple, original air, which, on account of the singularity of its source, may please some of your subscribers of that sex whose virtues, so often witnessed in my professional pursuits, I take pleasure in holding up to imitation.

"Sitting up one gloomy winter night with a poor gentleman who returned, after a long absence, to

172

finish his sickly remainder of life in an impoverished home, I heard the tale of early love, long deferred hope and disastrous fortunes, which I have told with more than poetic truth in the simple verses now sent to you. The good being who waited, welcomed and watched, has faithfully performed her promise, and he whom she loved in absence and unto death, has departed to a happier world, blessing with his last accents the angel hand of tireless and disinterested affection."

The verse of this, which directions say is to be played tenderly and with much feeling, runs:

> "I've waited long, but not in vain,
>   Though youth and health are gone;
> And days of sorrow, nights of pain,
>   Have found me still alone.
> I've waited long for thee,
>   And now thou comest back to me,
> With sorrow on thy furrow'd brow,
>   A wreck from fortune's sea."

The second verse is even more touching:

> "But welcome still, thou broken one,
>   Tho' nothing's left of thee,
> But that fair name and thrilling tone,
>   So dear of yore to me.

Tho' gone the flush of love's young day,
    Its calmer light will come,
To shed a purer, softer ray,
    On sorrow's stainless home."

There is also a "Song of the Tee-Totaller" written by Rev. Geo. W. Bethune, D. D., and running like this, *animato:*

"Let others praise the ruby bright
    In the red wine's sparkling glow,
But dear to me is the diamond light
    Of the fountain's clear flow;
The feet of earthly men have trod
    The juice from the bleeding vine,
But the stream comes pure from the
        hand of God
    To fill this cup of mine."

After every verse, the treble, alto, tenor and bass alternately sing as solos and finally in chorus the following:

"Then give me the cup of cold water!
The clear, sweet cup of cold water;
For his arm is strong tho' his toil be long,
Who drinks but the clear, cold water,
Who drinks but the clear, cold water."

Interesting also is the lisping comic song entitled "Wery Pekoolier," as sung by Mr. H. Russell and composed by J. Blewitt. There are five verses of

this and each verse has eleven lines. The refrain
goes thus:

"Wery perkoolier! tho' from that day to thith I have
   never
Theen or thpoken to her, but thomehow I can't help
   thinking—
Her behavior to me, it was wery perkoolier!!!"

"The Charming Woman," an "admired song,"
written by Mrs. Price Blackwood, recites the
charms of a certain Miss Myrtle who could read
both Latin and Greek and was said to have solved
a problem in Euclid before she could speak, but
Mrs. Blackwood, who evidently belonged to the old
school, deplored the fact that Miss Myrtle had
never been taught to hem and to sew, also that
she was "a little too thin" (it seemed that it was
possible to be too thin, then) and her dresses were
"nearly up to her knees." The moral which Mrs.
Blackwood draws is that no sensible man will ever
marry a charming woman.

The transformation in American music of which
jazz is the upshot started nearly twenty-five years
ago. Following the era of the popular ballad and
coon song, ten years later came ragtime.

Jazz

The best way I have found to differentiate between ragtime, blues and jazz is to indicate each by a line. The ragtime line is jerky. Blues has a long, easy line and the jazz line rises to a point. "The Maple Leaf" was the first rag. "Memphis Blues" was the first blues, so far as I have been able to find. The first was by Scott Joplin, the second by J. C. Handy. At least these were the earliest compositions that America called by the names of "ragtime" and "blues." Yet syncopation and rhythm which were the distinguishing marks of the ragtime were not really new. And when you added counterpoint and harmony to the melody and rhythm of ragtime, you got blues, essentially a trick of harmony. But the blues were not new, either. Can anybody who has ever heard it forget the distant shore in the opening of "Tristan and Isolde" which shimmers in a blue haze that one can feel?

At first both ragtime and blues were a sort of piano trick passed on from one performer to another. Up to the time that Handy organized an orchestra in Memphis, it is doubtful whether a single blue measure had ever been put on paper.

Handy wrote out the "blue" notes for the first time.

According to John Stark, publisher of ragtime in St. Louis, ragtime originally meant a negro syncopated dance, and the real negro blues were never intended as a dance at all, but were a sort of negro opera, more like a wail or a lament than anything else. Big sessions of blues were held in the South among the colored people, the biggest of all at "house rent stomps" when a negro found himself unable to pay his rent. The "stomp" consisted of a barbecue with music afterwards, during and before. The guests raised a purse to save their host's home and also composed a new blues for the occasion.

A high mark in popular musical history was "The Magic Melody" of Jerome Kern in 1915. This piece introduced a modulation which brought new harmonic richness and variety into American popular music where only stereotyped rhythms and melodies had been before. Mr. Kern was a real pioneer, for folks called the "Magic Melody" highbrow—terrible indictment in those days if you were earning your living writing music.

J a z z

Times and events have, of course, colored the evolution of both serious and popular music. Period songs mark the activities of a people. The pioneers and settlers sang hymns and folk songs. The Civil War brought a partisan type of song and the ballads of the Spanish-American wartime painted a country emotionally stirred, singing "There'll Be a Hot Time in the Old Town To-night" and "Break the News to Mother."

Jazz, which is ragtime and blues, combined with a certain orchestral polyphony which neither had, was still another way of letting off steam. At first, it was mainly rhythm running wild, tempos colliding with tempos. It is interesting to note that the earliest jazz was found uncopyrightable by certain judges. Interesting indeed are the reflections of Judge Carpenter in the District Court of Northern Illinois, Eastern Division, on October 14, 1917, in the case of LaRocca against E. Graham. A piece called "Barnyard Blues" and another called "Livery Stable Blues," which decidedly resembled each other, were involved in this copyright dispute.

Said the Judge: "This is a question of each

one claiming the right to this musical production. No claim is made by either side for the barnyard calls that are interpolated in the score, no claim is made for the harmony, the only claim seems to be for the melody. Now, as a matter of fact, the only value of this so-called musical production is the interpolated animal calls. These so-called animal sounds are not in question, are not claimed under the copyright. The only question is, whose brain conceived the idea of the melody that runs through the so-called 'Livery Stable Blues.' I am inclined to take the view of Professor White that this is an old negro melody which witness said he heard fifteen years ago. I think with Professor White that neither Mr. LaRocca nor Mr. Nunez conceived the idea of this melody. This band was a strolling band of players, none of them, according to the testimony, with a technical knowledge of music.

"This, of course, is not an essential to the production of pleasing or entertaining music. Take the Hungarian Strollers, with their wonderful music which has come down to us. They were untrained musicians in a technical way. So with this band. With a quick ear and a retentive memory, they hear,

179

remember and reproduce, and perhaps no living man could determine where that melody came from. What they produced was a result that pleased their patrons and it was the variations of the original music that accomplished the result, not the original music.

"I defy any living human being to listen to that production played upon the phonograph and discover any music in it, but there is a wonderful rhythm which in case you're a dancer and young, will set your feet moving."

So ended the first jazz controversy, also the first decision in regard to pilfered music. But the discussion was to be renewed. Which brings us to a catch question—are you bored by classical music? Does the very word "classical" make you nervous because it sounds so highbrowish? And do you, by chance, declare that jazz is the only kind of music you can possibly understand?

If the answer to all these questions is yes, the joke is really on you. For the truth is that, when you are listening to your favorite jazz tune, you are most likely absorbing strains that are most classic of all the classics. Do you not know that more than half the modern art of composing a popular song comes in knowing what to steal and how to adapt it—also, that at least nine-tenths of modern jazz music is turned out by Tin Pan Alley is frankly stolen from the masters?

That's why a good many of the jazzists chuckle over lowbrows who say they can't abide classical music and highbrows who squirm when they hear jazz. Pretty nearly everybody knows now that Händel's Messiah furnished the main theme of the well-known "Yes, We Have No Bananas." Perhaps it is not such general knowledge that most of the "banana" song which wasn't taken from the Messiah came from Balfe's famous "I Dreamt That I Dwelt in Marble Halls." Chopin supplied "Alice Blue Gown." "Avalon" was Tosca straight.

Chopin came into the limelight again with "I'm Always Chasing Rainbows," taken from the beautiful "Fantasie Impromptu Opus 66." The same master furnished the theme for "Irene." "If I Can't Get the One I Want" can be traced to Bach, if you are good at tracing things. "Marcheta" is reminiscent of the "Merry Wives of Windsor." "Iola" came from "The Blue Danube Waltz."

"Every Cloud Has a Silver Lining" more than suggests a Paderewski Minuet. "The Love Nest" is Tschaikowsky. "Russian Rose" is a frank adaptation of the "Volga Boat Song." Equally frank is the popular version of the "Song of India."

There is no legal limit to this kind of lifting, so long as the model chosen has not been copyrighted, and even then a few strategic notes changed by an expert can make everything quite safe. As to the moral aspects of the theft, there aren't any. There are, naturally, morals among musicians, but they aren't concerned with this question. All the music of the world is a kind of common storehouse, and Kipling expresses the musician's attitude toward it.

Not long ago, the heirs of a composer brought suit against a certain publishing house to recover damages for this kind of thieving. The publishing house produced in court the music to prove that the composer had himself taken his themes from the folk songs of several European countries. The composer's heirs lost their suit. The folk songs had never been copyrighted and were perfectly legitimate material for the composer—but also for the jazz musician.

Tin Pan Alley

It has never been a scandal in the musical world that the greatest composers of every period borrowed freely from each other. There is a nice little story told of Wagner and Liszt. They were listening together to one of Wagner's earliest rehearsals, when Wagner said, "Now you will hear something from your St. Elizabeth."

"Oh, well," replied Liszt, "then it will at least be heard."

There's a Händel story, too, that the composers of the "Banana" song ought to know. A friend pointed out to Händel that he had used the theme of a rival in his own works.

"Have I?" murmured Händel, carelessly. "It was much too good for him, anyway. He never knew what to do with it."

There is no question but that Händel knew what to do with the theme that was later to be jazzed into "Yes, We Have No Bananas." But Händel himself would no doubt have enjoyed the song that proved that the jazz musician knew what to do with it, too, in his own way.

This common use of muscial themes is so general that a hundred instances of it leap into the mind.

At random I may mention Tschaikowsky's use of the Marseillaise in his "1812 Overture" and Schubert's use of it in "The Two Grenadiers," the "Star Spangled Banner" in Puccini's "Madame Butterfly," Beethoven's borrowing of the "British Grenadier" in his "Septet Opus 20," and "The Campbells Are Coming" that romps gaily in Volkman's "Richard III Overture."

Still, even Congress has recently been stirred up about these customary predatory practices of composers. This was when Alfred E. Smith, representing the Music Industries of Commerce, appeared before the House Committee on Patents in Washington to oppose the measure in the new copyright bill which was intended to give every composer exclusive financial rights to his theme.

Why should they need protection, Mr. Smith wanted to know, when they themselves had always taken whatever they wanted, whenever they wanted it, wherever it was?

I suppose there will always be somebody dashing into courts of law to claim damages from some musician who is blithely following the usual custom of stealing good things here and there. An entertaining suit was that brought by a choir leader of Spokane, Wash., who wanted damages from an orchestra leader, on a general charge of syncopating the classics. The choir leader claimed that he suffered acute anguish because his artistic sensibilities were harrowed—although I don't know why he needed to listen to the orchestra—and that he sustained also a serious financial loss because children were having their musical taste perverted and no longer wanted real musical education.

As a matter of fact, even when an irate protector of the masters does get action to suppress certain music, it does him very little good. The reason for this is that music bootleggers have arisen who for a price will furnish the coveted orchestration to any leader who applies. The bootleg orchestration headquarters are rather like the ancient blind tigers of local option days. That is, they masquerade as pants-pressing establishments, junk shops or even, in extreme cases, the neighborhood drugstore which also supplies music to its patrons.

Well, bootleg or not, the jazz classical combination is really cultivating a taste for classical music.

185

At first glance this may seem strange. But it is true; and also it is natural enough. People grow familiar with the themes in jazz, their interest in music is stimulated by their love of jazz, and the natural next step is to follow the themes back toward their original sources. The original sources of musical themes are so far back in folk-song that it would probably be a lifetime job to trace only one. But just behind the jazz use of them is classical music.

Now, most Americans—for many reasons that I have already given—have been afraid of classical music. They were too humble; they thought they couldn't understand it. So they didn't try. They avoided classical music, and more or less scoffed at it. But when they come to it by way of jazz, they find it isn't so difficult to like it, and they do. They may not know all the highbrow musical jargon—which is, after all, only a technical vocabulary, just as a mechanic's special vocabulary is technical—but they do know what they like. And after all, music is written to be appreciated by the people, not to be argued about by critics.

This trend toward getting acquainted with classical music is a good thing. I should like to see every jazz record in every home in America accompanied by the record of the classical music from which the jazz theme was taken. I am all for it. The real lover of music likes jazz the better for knowing all music, just as he likes all music the better for knowing jazz. When I play a jazz version of "The Song of India," for instance, and learn that the effect of the sale of my record has been to increase the sales of the original record fifty per cent., I am delighted. The same thing happened after "Russian Rose" was put on the market; the public clamored for the beautiful record of "The Volga Boat Song." Instances of this kind are multiplying every day.

So it is no theory of mine that jazz is making America into a truly musical nation. There are facts and figures everywhere to prove it. The strange thing is the spectacle of the patrons of music in America, who for years have been keeping good music barely alive in this country by artificial stimulation, by maintaining splendid orchestras that had to be subsidized by the rich, while they lamented the lack of a musical public in this country. One would think they would rejoice, to see music rising like a wave and engulfing America, to see people music-mad. But a great many of them don't. Some of them raise their hands in horror, and say that jazz is vulgar. Well, it is, in the good old Latin sense of the word. It is vulgar; that is, it is the possession of the common people. As fast as sheet music can be printed, and phonograph records turned out, and little orchestras organized everywhere, classical music is becoming the possession of the American public, too. One thought that was what these music patrons wanted, all the time. But when every Tom, Dick and Harry takes to humming operas in this country, as Italian peasants do, will these lofty ones call the operas vulgar?

They should, to be consistent. But it's a strange world. Consistency may be a jewel; but most people would rather wear diamonds, even so.

IX

Tricks of the Trade

IX: Tricks of the Trade

*I*NVARIABLY, the layman is amused to discover that the saxophone and the banjo, both regarded by him as essentials to jazz, were not included in the original jazz band at all. As a matter of fact, the saxophone, which was invented more than seventy-five years ago by Antoine Sax, was designed as a very serious instrument. It was heard oftener in church than anywhere else and the story goes that Mendelssohn refused to allow it in his orchestra because it was too mournful!

The banjo is said to have been invented by a negro plantation hand from a cheese box. At any rate, it is strictly American and there are foreign instrument makers to-day, as well as perhaps some here at home who would consider that it is unworthy to be called a musical instrument if only there were not such a great demand for it.

The original jazz band consisted of a piano, a

trombone, a cornet, a clarinet and a drum. The fundamental harmony and rhythm were supplied by the piano, the player of which could usually read notes. The other performers had no notes, so it mattered not at all that they had never learned to read music. They simply filled in the harmonic parts and counter melodies by ear, interpolating whatever stunts in the way of gurgles, brays, squeals and yells occurred to them, holding up the entire tune, though still keeping in the rhythm.

The clarinetist devoted himself to the shrill upper notes of his instrument while the trombone and cornet were muted at will, or according to the ingenuity of their manipulator.

The drummer, meantime, would take shame to himself if at any one time he was working less than a dozen noisy devices.

Those days are gone forever or nearly so. Considered musically, the ideal orchestra is one which will contain a quartette of every kind of legitimate orchestral instrument, thus permitting a four-part harmony in every quality of musical tone. Although this does not prove entirely practical, it is still an ideal which every orchestra leader to-day sets for himself. The result, I will venture to say, is that the United States has a greater number of efficient economical, small orchestras than has ever been known anywhere.

The jazz orchestra of to-day differs from the symphony mainly in that the foundation of the symphony is its strings. All other instruments are added for tone color. In the jazz orchestra, the saxophone has been developed to take the place of the cello. In fact, it has been developed to such a high degree that it can be used for the foundation of the entire orchestra, taking the place of second violins, violas and cellos. The brasses then are used for contrast.

The wood winds, as the clarinet, form the basis of the military band. The jazz band then may be said to come somewhere in between the symphony and the military. We have computed that one baritone saxophone is equal in sonorousness to a section of nine or ten cellos; that one alto saxophone equals sixteen first violins or twelve seconds; that one tenor saxophone equals eight violas. That is why, with twenty-five men, including only eight first violinists and four saxophones we have been able to get the volume of an eighty piece symphony orchestra. At least Leopold Godowsky, famous pianist, has declared we have approximately that volume.

The saxophone, then, is, in a way, king of the jazz orchestra. Because of this, such demands have been made upon the saxophone player that the manufacturers of the instrument have had to develop it to meet the new needs. It was a very different product twenty, or even ten years ago, from what it is now. As a matter of fact, all instruments have been perfected in much the same way—that is, a demand for better tone quality and a more perfect scale has sprung up and the manufacturer has had to comply with the new specifications.

Some demon statistician has estimated that there are now 10,000,000 saxophone players in the world. The estimate probably falls far short of the reality. And those amateur music makers who are not playing the saxophone have taken to the banjo. They say some good genius always arises to meet any national need. Is it any wonder that the sound-proof apartment is now a glorious reality?

Tricks of the Trade

Musicians recognize four general classes of instruments in speaking of the orchestra—strings, wood winds, brasses, and the battery of traps, made up chiefly of instruments of percussion.

The legitimate strings include the violin, the viola, the violincello and the double bass. To this may be added a few such instruments as the viol da gamba and the viol d'amore. Other strings stand in a musical sense midway between these and the instruments of percussion. These other strings include the piano, cymbalon, harp and a vast number of the mandolin, banjo, guitar and ukelele family. Of these, my orchestra has eight first violins, two pianos, a banjo and a cymbalon.

Wood wind instruments include, first of all the flute, which has many forms such as the piccolo or octave-flute, the bass flute, the Hungarian and Chinese flutes, the fife, the flageolet or tin whistle, and half the pipes of the ordinary pipe organ. Among the wood winds are the oboe family which takes in all instruments having a double reed—the oboe itself, the musette, the oboe d'amore, the cor anglaise or English horn, the heckelphone or baritone oboe, and the bassoon or contrabassoon.

The sarrusophone, which is made in seven or more sizes, is named with the wood winds although it is metal. For this reason, it is sometimes mistakenly called a metal oboe. The clarinet family, which includes all the single reed wood wind instruments, has the clarinet in various keys, the bassett horn, the bass clarinet, the heckelcarind and similar instruments, besides the saxophones in all keys, which, like the sarrusophone are made of metal. The Highland bagpipe belongs to both the single and double reed classes. Among the reeds should also be put the reed or cabinet organ, sometimes called a harmonium, the accordion, the mouth organ or harmonica, and many of the pipes of the pipe organ.

Of the wood winds, my orchestra has four saxophones—that is, four saxophone players, but all of these play saxophones in various keys—clarinet, oboe, English horn, heckelphone, octavon, accordion and piccolo.

Brasses include the trumpet, the cornet in its various forms, the trombone, either valved with a simple slide or with a complicated combination of slides and valves, the French horn, which in symphony is classed with the wood wind instruments; the alto and tenor horns; the baritone horn, or euphonium; the tuba and contra-bass tuba; the Bayreuth-tuba; the contra-bass horn; the bugle; the coach horn; the saxhorn or keyed bugle, made in seven or more sizes, and a number of others. Of the brasses, we have the trumpets, trombones, French horns and tubas.

The battery of an orchestra includes so many instruments that if one were to try to name them all, the list would stretch from here into infinity. The truth is, almost anything capable of making sound may be introduced into the battery for special effects. Thus, if one wants thunder and lightning, rain, hail, pistol shots, cuckoo calls, the cackling of a chicken, or the crying of a baby, one relies upon the traps player to produce it. Perhaps the most important instruments of the battery are the tympani or kettle drums, the side or snare drums, the bass drum, the tambourine, the triangle, cymbals, tom-tom, Chinese drum, castenets, rattle, glockenspiel and celesta, xylophone, marimba and bones. Of these, we have the celesta, two tympani, snare and bass drum and dozens of fixings for our special effects.

It is rather hard to classify the performers in any jazz orchestra, for the reason that most of the players perform on many different instruments. Thus with twenty-five players, we have more than forty instruments. Doubling is, then, the main strength of the jazz orchestra, making it possible to get the maximum of volume and color with the minimum of men.

For convenience, I shall summarize the instruments of my orchestra: eight first violins, two pianos, one banjo, a cymbalon, a celesta, two B-flat trumpets, two trombones, two French horns, two tubas, two tympani, snare and bass drum, all the traps, an oboe, an English horn, a heckelphone, four saxophones in B-flat soprano, E-flat alto, B-flat tenor, E-flat baritone; clarinets—B-flat base, E-flat alto, B-flat alto, E-flat baritone, B-flat tenor; octavon; piccolo; accordion and flute.

The four saxophone players double on all the single and double reed instruments. The second pianist doubles on the celesta. One of my clarinet players not only plays the clarinet in all keys, but doubles also on the oboe, the piccolo and the flute. The string bass player doubles on the tuba, one violin player doubles on the accordion and I've seen one man in the course of an evening play as many as twelve instruments, including three saxophones, three clarinets, the oboe, the octavon, the heckelphone, the xylophone and bagpipes.

So far, this seems to me a fairly satisfactory concert jazz orchestra. We are always trying out new instruments and discarding old ones, so that I don't feel we shall ever be satisfied to grow static. For a dance orchestra, eight violins are an unnecessary number of strings. Also, one of the pianos may be omitted and an extra banjo added. At one time, I tried out the organ for a dance orchestra, but found it too heavy and overpowering for the kind of music we make. Another instrument we have used is the harp which gives a pleasant effect in certain pieces, but is not useful enough to make it worth having in the average small orchestra. In the double reeds, I am planning to add a bassoon.

Jazz players have become so adept at handling their instruments that they nearly make each do the work of two. The tricks of the trade rapidly become public property, especially if they are put on the records. Thus the discoveries go East and West, North and South, to enrich orchestras in remote spots. Many jazz conductors and arrangers can adapt an orchestration from hearing a record played. I have heard some of our arrangements which bands had obtained in that way and they were well played, too. Such adaptation needs, however, a good musical ear and considerable technical knowledge. I am told that when a record is made by certain Eastern orchestras, arrangers of orchestras in the West and Middle West gather for the first playing with paper and pencil.

The various stunts with mutes, while pretty well known to those in the business, are important enough to speak of in some detail. The chief kinds of mutes are made of metal and cardboard. Before clever manufacturers saw the possibilities of these bits of material, the players themselves were using ingenious contrivances to get the same effects.

The first time I ever heard what I call the wawa mutes, used with the cornet, was, I think, when we did "Cut Yourself a Piece of Cake." The players got that effect by inverting glass tumblers over the bells of the instruments.

Did you ever see a kazoo? Of course you must have—a small worthless-looking piece of tin. A kazoo stuck into a mute will give a buzzy sound that comes handy in certain pieces.

In spite of the new appliances, hats, preferably derbies, are still used for mutes. When hung over the instrument, these give a French horn effect—that is, fuller quality and softer tone. A soft hat, having no resonant power, is no good for this purpose. The humble tin can is useful to give a big, open, and rather harsh tone. The aluminum or copper mute gives a sweeter tone and the pressed paper or cardboard mute is softer than any of the metal, but rather sharp in tone. A kazoo in the end of a cardboard mute gives an effect almost like an oboe. A cup-shaped brass mute gives a shallow tone with a thin quality. The flutter tongue in the brasses is rather like a covey of quail flying out from ambush.

One of our trombonists has a special mute such as I have never seen before, by which he gets a beautiful graduation of sound very like the voice of a sweet human baritone singer. In the case of most cup-shaped mutes, the air goes in and comes out the same way, but with this one, the air goes from one chamber into another and out. This player makes his vibrato with his lower lip. This takes, of course, a well-trained lower lip, and practice combined with natural aptitude is the only recipe I know to recommend.

Horn players can sharpen their instruments a whole or half tone by using their hands. This again has to be worked out by practice into a technique all a player's own.

The glissando is one of the chief embellishments of jazz. This is simply a sliding together of the chromatic scale. That is, instead of fingering the scale, the player slurs the tones together rapidly. Performers with brasses and reeds, especially if the reeds are flexible, get a weird effect and add to the rhythm by this trick. A glissando on the clarinet at the opening of the "Rhapsody in Blue" has attracted a great deal of attention. This trick takes a lip that is well trained. Again, practice, and I might say, a naturally obedient set of muscles, will do the job. The wawa effect on reeds can be gotten simply by blowing into the mouthpiece. Slap tonguing is accomplished by sucking on the reed, thus creating a vacuum, then hitting the vacuum with the tongue, causing a pop.

Jazz makes frequent use of the staccato on the violin by playing near the frog of the bow. The violins also do glissando in double stops. The kazoo effect, by the way, was original with us and we tried to disguise it for a while but were soon found out. The jazz band is always busy with new tricks. The drummer used to have to originate most of the sounds. Now every man in the orchestra tries to outdo him. Some of the effects depend upon very small things. Indeed, a tiny mute gives a neater sound than a large mute which is what we call rather "sloppy."

One interesting device used with the trombone I must mention. This is achieved by holding the bell of the instrument to the small end of a phonograph horn, with a result that has almost the qualities of a baritone voice. The saxophone, to my way of thinking, can come the nearest of any instrument to reproducing the human masculine voice. The clarinets are equally adept in trained hands of simulating the feminine voice. Both brass and wood winds can produce laughter that is uncannily realistic.

Some trick stuff is all right and some is in the very worst possible taste. For instance, a man who wires a mouth organ to his face as a solo instrument and uses the piano to accompany himself is making himself ridiculous. If your trick stuff is clever, use it. If not, keep away.

One of the qualities in the musician that the jazz orchestra has developed is ingenuity. If he feels that he needs a certain sound from his instrument, he puts his hand or his foot in it or goes and gets a beer bottle, if nothing else is at hand.

The orthodox have, I think, been pretty well shocked by the employment of curious devices for altering the tonal quality of certain ancient and respected instruments. Somebody has suggested that this is because the mechanism is often rather baldly exposed. With the new mutes, perhaps, this will eventually be improved. As a matter of fact, not nearly all the jazz stunts are new. For instance, the derby mute of the clarinet goes back to 1832 when Hector Berlioz directed the clarinetist at a certain passage in his "Lelio ou le Retour à la Vie," to wrap the instrument in a leather bag to "give the sound of the clarinet an accent as vague and remote as possible."

The glissando of the trombone occurs in the orchestral score of Schoenberg's "Pelleas et Melisande," written in 1902 when jazz was as yet entirely unknown. Schoenberg is also the father of the flutter on the trombone—that is, very rapid tonguing on the same note. And Stravinsky, in the days when jazz was still in its infancy, used muted trumpets.

Yet jazz has developed much that is new and this is its chief service to music. Music, like everything else, gets static in its development during any period when fresh tools are not being devised. From the way in which some of the jazz devices have been received, one might think that it was lese majesty to make a pleasing sound in any way in which it had not been made before. Yet the development of music has gone hand in hand with the development of new instruments from the day when the first savage found that hitting a hollow log with a club made a sound that stirred human emotions.

There is a story somewhere to the effect that the man who first strung a board with catgut and made sounds upon it was put to death because his fellow men resented the introduction of a new noise into a world which they regarded as already overstocked with sounds. So you see, there have always been cranks and reformers.

The jazz band has introduced some little-known instruments such as the heckelphone, the slide cornet and the czimbalon. It has developed such new ones as the sarrusophone. And, of course, the banjo has received so much attention that it would hardly be surprising to hear of it being taken into the symphony. The now notorious saxophone, in almost any of its sizes and keys, is one of the most useful of modern instruments. It is easy to learn —I believe there is a tradition that an ambitious boy can get the hang of it in twenty minutes—but difficult to master. But other instruments are still more difficult to master, and what is more, it is not necessary to master the saxophone to play dance music.

JEANNE GORDON, OF THE METROPOLITAN OPERA, CROWNING
THE KING OF JAZZ

Tricks of the Trade

Saxophones supply the element of humor which American dancers insist upon having and they are also extremely flexible so that more or less difficult running passages may be played with ease. In skilled hands, then, the saxophone is capable of smooth intonation in solo passages, though like all reeds, the control of pitch is not easy.

With two or three saxophones for the same player, one may obtain a large variety of tone effects, shifting a melody into the deep bass with good effect, and then by picking up a smaller instrument, obtaining a cold blue tone almost as pure as that of the flute. Or, as they do in England, one may take the little top sax, and push it up to super-acute register to make extremely funny noises.

The collective compass of the soprano, alto, tenor and baritone saxophones is a little more than four octaves, so there is sufficient territory for the complete performance of many pieces without the use of any other instruments.

As the basis for a three-piece orchestra, the saxophone is thoroughly successful. One combination possible is the saxophone, xylophone and piano. Offhand, one might think there would be too much percussion and too little melody, but a baritone saxophone is beautifully set off by the sparkle of the xylophone and the piano holds together the rhythm.

Strictly speaking, there are no more three-piece orchestras. In a modern orchestra, two men often play a dozen instruments and three men, provided they are equipped with the right number of instruments, can turn themselves into a huge working force.

The best one-man dance orchestra is and always has been the piano. Nine-tenths of the music in the civilized world has been written for this old stand-by and practically all arrangeable music has been arranged for it. And the best piano orchestra is the piano alone!

The banjo, going on to the next typical instrument, is the instrument of highest importance in our type of orchestra. Its tone is clear, snappy, and it carries farther even than that of the piano. It is capable of rhythmic and harmonic effects that a leader is put to it to find in any other instrument.

You can get more pizzicato effects, you can get relatively greater volume with a single banjo than you can with a whole symphony load of pizzicato violins and violas and you can play passages they wouldn't dare to attempt. There is an example in a piece we used to be fond of playing, "On the Sip, Sip, Sippy Shore," where "Turkey in the Straw" is introduced as a banjo solo. The pace is furious and the swift and flexible hands of the artist must move fast indeed. What symphony conductor would dare put such a passage as this in the hands of his pizzicato strings? Yet the single instrument, in the dance orchestra, with one set of fingers, is all that is required.

In the ensemble, the banjo may be considered even more important than as a solo instrument. If the banjo is a good timekeeper, it will tone down the piano, stop the traps from banging and cause the whole organization, no matter how many instruments there are, to move on the beat like one man.

Obviously, the jazz band has tried to develop extreme sounds. The deepest, the most piercing and the softest effects are produced but any jazz orchestra leader will soon learn that he gets his best effects if he plays softly. It is not necessary to bang to get your effect or to burst the instrument for volume. On the contrary, a good jazz orchestra is at its best and most seductive when at its quietest.

The tubists give the bass notes an effective soft definiteness while the muted brasses and high-pitched saxophones and clarinets provide the excitement and color.

The early jazz was each man for himself and devil take the harmony. The demoniac energy, the fantastic riot of accents and the humorous moods have all had to be toned down. I hope that in toning down we shall not, as some critics have predicted, take the life out of our music. I do not believe we shall. It seems to me that we have retained enough of the humor, rhythmic eccentricity, and pleasant informality to leave us still jazzing. And while we do not have so much unrestricted individualism as in the old days, every man must still be a virtuoso.

A critic has said that if jazz is to rise to the level of musical art, it must overthrow the government of the bass drum and the banjo and must permit itself to make excursion into the regions of elastic rhythms. Perhaps that is true. All I know is that if somebody will write us a different kind of music, we shall be glad to try to play it. So far the jazz orchestra is the only typically American arrangement of instruments that has ever been made. The brass band has been done in this country very well, but not with original instrumentation. Never before has the combination of saxophone, brass, banjo, piano, drums and little strings been tried.

As I have tried to indicate, the modern jazz orchestra is an efficient arrangement. Every member knows exactly what he is to play every minute of the time. Even the smears are indicated in the music. Rehearsals are as thorough and frequent as in any symphony. The discipline of the orchestra, if it is a good one, must be complete. Yet there must be freedom such as I have never seen in any symphony. The men must get joy out of their work. They must have a good time and try to give their audience one.

Music is human. The character of the man that handles the instrument shows in his music just as his character shows in his handwriting. Every

211

human being has his own value, his own character. It is when this variety is released into music that music strives and grows. Jazz has forever ended the time when music was—to the average American —a series of black and white notes on white paper, to be learned by rote and played according to direction in a foreign language—staccato, legato, crescendo.

Jazz has taught Americans that they may take any old thing that will make a sound that pleases them and please themselves by expressing with it their own moods and characters in their own rhythms, thus making music. The saxophone, in spite of the fact that at one time it was used for church music, comes romping into the orchestra like a wild Westerner into Boston society. Even the tin pan is not to be despised just because it was made originally to hold milk. Says jazz, put an old hat over a trumpet and make it sing as it never sang before. Who cares that it is only an old hat.

It was, after all, some very distinguished persons who started putting base agencies to work when they needed them. Schubert used to amuse his friends by wrapping tissue paper around a comb and singing the "Erlking" through it, and Tschaikowsky required the same implement to get his effects in the "Dance of the Mirlitons." The highly respected orchestras of the seventies employed cannon that broke all the crockery for miles around when they wished to get the effect of a battle.

Also, the jew's-harp a century ago was regarded as a highbrow instrument, Eulenstein playing sixteen at once before the King of England and getting a decoration for it. To be sure, the musician's teeth broke off one by one before he ended his career, the last with such a clatter that he was literally thrown out of court. But that's no argument against America making a joyful noise with whatever she has nearest at hand!

213

X

Orchestration

X: Orchestration

*T*HE secret of the success of modern dance music is in its arrangement. For unless the music is cleverly scored, the greatest musicians cannot make it popular with the public.

Any man who is planning a career as a musician ought to know how to transpose at sight. Every score that comes to me is analyzed and dissected at rehearsal, down to the very last note. Naturally, the small orchestra arrangement will not always fit, so I take the music apart phrase by phrase and find just where each melody lies according to the possibility of each instrument.

Did you ever stop to consider that a single note on some trap instrument will carry away with it as much memory as thirty bars of senseless pounding?

Jazz orchestrations have done more to change the character of the jazz orchestra than anything else. The distribution of the music has been made definite, a balance has been kept between the choirs. The arranger distributes the parts to his orchestra and here all his knowledge and wit are demanded. Mr. Grofe considers the orchestra a sort of quartette, ranging from soprano to bass. In the separate instrumental groups, he also divides the parts from high to low. If you give the highest voice and the lowest to the saxophone and the middle voices to the brass, you will get a singularly rich effect of having three or four times more than the saxophones you are using. If you give the high voice and the low to the brass and fill in the middle with the saxophone, you will get the opposite effect.

Perhaps it would be interesting to show what actually happens to a simple melody when made ready for the use of a jazz orchestra. Suppose we take the popular song, "Oh, Katharina." The orchestrator in this case, the talented Frank Barry, decided to put in German atmosphere, therefore starts with a little "Ach Du Lieber Augustine." The first verse is left fairly straight and the first chorus is done in the regular American manner so as to "set" the tune.

Then comes a half chorus in jazz. After that starts some counterpoint with a German tune. The saxophones are changed to the oboe and clarinets playing the melody while the tuba plays "In Tiefen Keller," the famous German drinking song. The brass and saxophones then play the melody staccato while the violins play the "Soldier's Farewell," a German folk song.

The piece now softens down to muted brasses playing the melody while the solo clarinet plays "Hi Lee Hi Lo" for a half chorus, then with trumpet fanfare modulates into "Oh Tannenbaum" while the violins and saxophones try to make themselves heard with the melody. A half chorus of hot jazz and then the strains of "Ach, Du Lieber Augustine" bring the orchestration to a close.

The main point in such orchestration is that after the tune is set the instrumentation shall be changed for each half chorus. In between, the keys are shifted, with a four to eight bar interlude to get into the new key. The new demand is for change and novelty. Four years ago, a whole chorus could be run through with but one rhythmic idea. Now

there must be at least two rhythmic ideas and sometimes more.

On the other hand, it is necessary to avoid over-
crowding with material, for the melody must not
be lost. "Noodles," that is, fancy figures in saxophone such as triple trills, often crowd out the melody, and the point to remember is that everything
else is secondary to keeping this alive.

XI
On Wax

XI: On Wax

*W*HEN our first records came down from the laboratories of the Victor Company for their initial "audition," a visitor exploded, "What the dickens?"

Then he listened to a few bars—he was an experienced listener—and demanded: "Who is it?"

The one step was dying a natural death and in that death was becoming apotheosized into the fox trot. But our first record was different from either. Perhaps dancers in America who are old enough will remember it. It was a twelve-inch disc, the first I think of the dance variety ever made that size, and there was a one step on one side of it arranged from the "Dance of the Hours." On the other, was the legally immortalized "Avalon" which gave occupation for a time to the copyright lawyers of two continents under the theory that it had been plagiarized from "La Tosca." This was one of the greatest fox trots of the late "glide" period.

The companion record was that masterpiece of dance composition "The Japanese Sandman," ranking with the earlier "Havanola," which Rudolph Gans had had scored by the composer and played by the St. Louis Symphony Orchestra as an example of American music. The even more popular "Whispering" was on the other side.

For years before we began to record, it had been necessary for almost all recording laboratories to change the instrumentation of nearly all orchestral pieces. Certain instruments, notably the double basses, which were then used, the horn, the tympani, and in lesser degree, other instruments, failed to yield satisfactory results. The double basses frequently were discarded and replaced by a single tuba. Modifications also in the placing of the orchestra were necessary in order to make the volume of tone from a large number of instruments converge upon a tiny diaphragm whose vibrating needle inscribed, upon a disc of wax, the mysterious grooves, which, retraced by a second needle attached to a second diaphragm, gave back the voices and accents of music.

So for all our labor and study, we had to go into the recording room and learn all over. One of the changes we made when we found that ordinary drums could not be put on the record was to use the banjo as a tune drum. The tympani and snare drum record, but the regular drum creates a muddy and fuzzed-up effect when other music is going, although solo drums make very good records. It was at this time that I tried out the banjo for the ground rhythm and discovered the possibilities of that small instrument which until then had been kept in the back and hardly heard at all. We also discovered that almost every instrument has a treacherous or bad note and that when the score calls for that note the instrument had better stop playing. An extreme dissonance would mean that the record would be blasted. For all our troubles, however, we were told that fewer changes had to be made in our scoring than in any dance records of the time. As a rule we made two records at a time, though once I believe we made nine in three days. Each record averages about an hour and a half or two hours, for there must first be a rehearsal and a test before the perfect record is passed upon by the company "hearing committee."

Recording is perhaps the most difficult task in the day's work—or the lifetime's. A slip may pass unnoticed in concert, whether across the footlights or over the radio, and even if noticed, it may be forgiven, since living flesh and sensitive will cannot always achieve mechanical perfection. But a slip in a record after a time becomes the most audible thing in it. Everything else will be neglected to wait for the slip and to call the attention of some one else uninstructed in music to a great artist's false note. So every composition has to be recorded until it is perfect. If things go fine from the first, well and good; but if, from the three records of each number usually made, there is none which will quite pass the exacting standards of the committee, there must be another afternoon of making and remaking. Every faculty of the artist, emotional as well as physical, must be expended in producing a perfect result.

In late recording practice, with highly improved methods of capturing sound and with new scientific

principles, it has grown more and more practicable
to record large bodies of instruments without losing
volume, without having a large quantity of tone
dilute and diffuse itself before reaching the actual
path of the recording apparatus.

In the laboratory, as we worked, the possibilities
of the orchestra began to loom large and the original plan with a single player for each type of
instrument began to expand. The saxophone, for
instance, had always had a shadow or understudy.
A third saxophone now was added and in time the
orchestra developed the full Wagnerian quartette
of instruments in this group. The one trumpet was
reinforced by a second and the now popular combination "straight" and "comedy" trumpets came
into existence. The banjo instead of just marking
time began to make new excursions into the realms
of rhythm and the fox trot began to change without, however, disturbing the pedestrian order of
things.

Not all these changes took place, of course, in
the laboratory. Most of the rehearsing and discussing and rescoring was done in consultations
outside—consultations not always free of the heat

of argument. The actual business of recording is a star chamber matter but it is no violation of a secret to admit that some of our early records were spoiled by men swearing softly at themselves before they learned the new adroitness which the delicate mechanism of the recording room required.

The records of our orchestra that I have liked particularly are fox trots like the "Song of India," with its burst of two part harmony, the "Waters of the Minnetonka," with its wood wind accompanimental figure and its swinging climax and the insidiously delicate "Oh, Joseph."

One sees all one's friends and some of one's enemies at the recording laboratories and the exchange of experience between the classicist and "coonshouter," the string quartette and the clarinet jazz band is illuminating for everybody.

Not long ago, Rosa Ponselle, Mischa Elman and I were all recording at the Victor, though in different laboratories. We had lunch together and regardless of the fact that the temperature was above 90, the great dramatic soprano demonstrated a dance step for us in the best Broadway style. Then we sat for our pictures, she in her bungalow

apron, Elman minus collar and coat and I in plus
four knickerbockers.

It interested me that the singer should have been
familiar with the current fox trot step, for with the
almost weekly changes in the dance I had begun to
believe that only orchestra leaders and college boys
could possibly keep pace. We have even to antici-
pate the change and that has become our chief
problem as the public is well aware. Dancers and
musicians, as a rule, are harder to bring together than
the various labor unions working on a big building. Ballroom dancers persistently refuse to con-
form to accepted or classical styles, or to any styles
which they do not determine for themselves in the
ballrooms of the hour. Any study of the long list
of our fox trots will reveal peculiarities in tempo,
rhythm and general style not to be accounted for
on the basis of "individual variation," or the time-
honored principle that "nature makes no two faces
alike"; the simple truth of the matter is, that a
dance, almost, is no sooner in the hands of the
public than the style changes.

During the past half-dozen years there have been
several powerfully marked variations in the ordi-

nary, or "two-step" fox trot. The original "glide two-step" fox trot of the "Japanese Sandman" period soon was succeeded by the "radio roll" or the "scandal walk" (the two passed into one another) by the "blues," which was officially earlier but in point of fact later in the experience of many dancers than the "collegiate," which set up an entirely new style of dancing and called for an entirely new type of music. The "tango fox trot" prevailed in a few cities, the "military fox trot," and entirely local dances with fanciful, and in some cases meaningless, names, in others.

All of these changes of style or local and individual caprices in taste, have to be ministered to by a dance organization as large as ours, or we soon perish. Few new dances, except those for stage use, are ever brought forward by teachers; they are developed, in public, by persons of no particular skill, and with little or no knowledge of the dance as an art. It is avowed, and on excellent authority, that the "collegiate" sprang from the use of rubber-soled summer footwear and slow, sticky dance floors at public resorts, where the skate-like slides and pivots of the old-style dancer were impossible. With footwear of this sort it was possible to do little else than stamp up and down. From this developed a polka-like dance with crude hops and jumps, calling for agility, but with no great degree of sophisticated grace.

Small items like this determine the whole power of survival of an orchestra. When a method crystallizes or a dance is standardized, it is done. For the younger generation everywhere who invented it, without half knowing most of the time what they were about, are now through with it.

One phenomenon I noted when I was playing dance music at the Palais Royal on Broadway. A fox trot was played in a rhythm exactly that of the Habanera or Tango, but much swifter in time. The result was that the easy "chasse" skips peculiar to this type of dance became impossible to the dancers who thereby changed their rhythm from that of the tango to the easier two-step with the result that six hundred fox-trotters—not all of whom could be charged with profound musical knowledge—automatically were dancing in cross rhythm.

XII

Jazz Makers

XII: Jazz Makers

I HAVE a friend and you probably know
somebody just like him who, when it's time
for the salad at dinner, immediately rolls up his
sleeves and wades merrily into the job of shaking
reluctant oil and vinegar into friendly combination
whilst tobasco, paprika and other favorite condi-
ments wait their turn on the sidelines. The process
of mixing salad dressing as done by Jim always re-
minds me of making a jazz band.

The ingredients have to be just so—everything
cold, the oil perfectly fresh, the vinegar not too
tart and yet tart enough. But the real art comes in
putting in just enough of everything and not the
bit too much that will turn the mixture sour or oily
or peppery.

So it is with a jazz orchestra. There must be
no staleness, no luke-warmness, no over or under
seasoning. It is not so easy to mix either a good

dressing or a good jazz band. Conventional measurements are of no use for the goal is individuality—yet not an odious individuality such as comes with a dressing too spicy for the common palate or an orchestra where there are so many stars that the blend is not rich and smooth.

The first essential of any good orchestra is musicians of the very first water. But with a jazz orchestra, this is not nearly enough. Jazz players must be masters, not merely of one, but several instruments, so that a small group can produce the tone and color of a far larger one by doubling on two, three or half a dozen instruments.

Jazz players have to possess not merely musical knowledge and talent but musical intelligence as well. In a symphony, the conductor is the personality which stands out. In a jazz orchestra, every man is more or less in the limelight. Therefore each man must be clever enough to sell himself to the audience—in other words, he must be a good showman.

He must have initiative, imagination and inventiveness amounting almost to genius. In the symphony, the composer invents. With us, that job falls to the player. This versatile individual must be young enough that the spirit of adventure is still in him. He must be temperamental enough to feel and not too temperamental to be governed. Neatness in dress and a cheerful expression are important assets and a sense of humor is practically indispensable. A jazz player must be inherently optimistic. He will never get over in our business if he pulls a long, solemn face. It is better to be overly irresponsible than overly serious-minded if a man takes up jazz-making for a living.

Perhaps the most important item in the jazz equipment is that each player shall be American. It is better to be a native-born American and better still, if one's parents were born here, for then one has had the American environment for two generations and that helps a great deal in playing jazz. At least, the musician must be a naturalized citizen, which means a considerable residence and a knowledge of language and customs.

My men are of every kind of ancestry—Italian, German, French, English, Scandinavian. That does not matter. Nor does their religion, of which there are almost as many varieties as there are men.

Jazz

What does matter is that they are all American citizens and nearly all native-born. Most of them are married. I prefer them so, not that married men are better jazzers, especially, but they are more conscientious and stick to their jobs with greater persistence.

I got a good many of my twenty-five men from symphonies. One of these is Walter Bell who plays the bass and contra-bassoon. He played in the San Francisco symphony and has written two or three symphonies himself. He got his start playing the mandolin and guitar in an ice cream parlor where the mice and rats were so thick that he had to keep his feet up on a table to prevent the pests gnawing the leather of his shoes.

It was through him that I really got to know and like jazz and I picked him for my own orchestra (mentally and provisionally, of course, because in those days I was lucky to have a job) at a performance of the Symphony in San Francisco. Bell was regularly playing bass but the bassoon got sick and I being the youngest member of the orchestra, was chased off to bring his instrument down for Bell to play.

He played it, and beautifully, but right in the midst of the 6th Tschaikowsky Symphony, he commenced to play in all off-rhythms—jazz really. I don't know why he did it—just a crazy impulse, I suppose, to shock the staid symphony and curiosity to see how his experiment would sound—or hear how it would sound, rather. Nobody paid much attention except myself and I felt like applauding, it was so well done.

Another man who came to us from a symphony is Chester Hazlett, also of the San Francisco group. He was a first clarinet at seventeen in a symphony, but he plays the saxophone for us because that's the instrument he likes best.

Frank Siegrist, trumpeter, and I played together in the Navy and experienced together some of the difficulties of trying to supply eight orchestras to as many company commanders when we only had the makin's of four. But discipline was discipline in the Navy and nothing was impossible (that's a Navy slogan), so we always made up the eight orchestras out of something.

It was of Siegrist that Alfred Hertz, conductor of the San Francisco Symphony, said: "I don't believe there is another lip like that trumpeter's anywhere in the world! What I wouldn't give if I could have a man like that! But of course you, with all the money you make, can afford to pay him more than a symphony ever could!"

"Well," said I, for I couldn't resist the opportunity to rub it in a little, "you might have had this man, for he tried out for you no less than four times before I got him and you turned him down every time!"

Mr. Hertz is one of the many real musicians who have changed their sentiment about jazz. When he first heard me jazz a classic (it was the "Peer Gynt" suite) he was frantic. He said he hoped I'd have to "sleep on snakes, snails and worms" to pay me out for the sacrilege, but when we went to San Francisco the last time, he called his orchestra together and introduced me with a flattering speech.

Henry Busse, also a trumpeter, is another symphony man. He has played in a number of the high-class musical organizations of Germany and knows the classics thoroughly. Yet it was he who stuck a kazoo in a regular mute one day (he got the kazoo from a ten-cent store across the street) and got an

Oriental quality like an oboe that I had been wanting for a long time.

Men taken from symphonies are the easiest to train. They have had good discipline and they usually leave the symphony because they are interested in jazz and want to experiment along a new line. Their knowledge of music is valuable and they know their instruments. The real blues player is more hidebound in his way than the symphony man. Blues become almost a religion and the man who worships them thinks nobody who can really play them is ever able to read music.

I had a New Orleans boy, Gus Miller, who was wonderful on the clarinet and saxophone, but he couldn't read a line of music. I tried to teach him, but he wouldn't try to learn, so I had to play everything over for him and let him get it by ear. I couldn't understand why he was so lazy or stubborn or both. He said he was neither.

"It's like this," he confided one day. "I knew a boy once down in N'Awleens that was a hot player, but he learned to read music and then he couldn't play jazz any more. I don't want to be like that."

A little later, Gus came to say he was quitting. I was sorry and asked what was the matter. He stalled around a while and then burst out:

"Nuh, Suh, I jes' can't play that 'pretty music' that you all play. And you fellers can't never play blues worth a damn!"

I have paid a good jazz player as much as $30,000 a year and none of the good ones get less than $200 a week. Many get $250 and $300. This is good pay, but then a well-trained, well-advertised jazz orchestra demands good money and gets it.

I choose my men according to the characteristics I have already set down and I find them everywhere. Many of them come to me for try-outs. We have forty or fifty applications for jobs every day in the New York office. My friends, too, scout around for me and, naturally, I hear every orchestra I can, everywhere I go. I catalogue the likely players and some day when I have a vacancy, I reach for the person who seems likely to fill the place. I always have plenty of names on file, for the music business is just like any other. A doctor will recommend a doctor in another town to you if you are moving away from his section and music men recommend cornetists and saxophonists in the same way.

Our rehearsals are free for alls. Every man is allowed to give his ideas, if he has any, about how new pieces should be played. The orchestra makes a kind of game of working out effects that will go. In shirt sleeves, if it's hot, and in bathing suits if it's hotter, with sandwiches and cold drinks handy, we've been known to forget quitting time by several hours.

When we are about to do a new piece, Grofe, my arranger, and I spend several hours discussing it from every point. Then, if we are in a hurry for it, he takes two days to arrange it, working often night and day. Sometimes he keeps right on for three or four days without any sleep. The initial rehearsal requires only about thirty-five or forty minutes, owing to Grofe's skill and the ease with which the boys pick up new numbers. That is, after forty minutes' practice, we are ready to play a new piece —one that has the typical jazz effects of mutes and special parts.

There is very little prima donna stuff in my orchestra, in spite of the proficiency of each man. We all work together for what we are trying to do. Star stuff can spoil any group. Coöperation can make even a mediocre band go great. If any one of the boys gets an inspiration, we stop and try it out. Some of the suggestions prove, when tried, to be no good, but I'd far rather have enthusiastic youth and a few mistakes in my orchestra than seasoned, too careful old stagers. The appeal of the jazz orchestra comes from spontaneity rather than from finished, brainy work. And for spontaneity, one needs wholesale youth.

The men are as enthusiastic over a new method or a new instrument as I am. When a queer-shaped contraption that somebody has dug up is brought in, everybody crowds around and wants to try it. The boys are always experimenting with fresh combinations, hoping to nose out a new bit of business. I wouldn't have a stolid man in my orchestra. The audience would feel a lack instantly. I think I'd fire a man quicker any day for a show of really surly disposition than for a serious mistake in musical execution.

Not but what my boys may lose their tempers

occasionally if they find it necessary. A fit of temperishness once in a while is natural enough and comes with temperament. Perhaps I shall be criticized for allowing temperament on my list. I believe, however, that all who do creative work are blessed or cursed with temperament. It seems to be a way nature provides for balancing excessive strain. Of course it can be carried to rather extraordinary extremes.

A musical comedy star I know invariably kicks and screams when she comes off the stage after an evening's work. But at other times she is a very good-humored little person. Once in Denver, a hotel waiter told me that he had spent most of the morning offering eggs to De Pachmann, the musician. It seemed, he wanted two eggs that matched and he sent back nearly a dozen pairs before he got two yolks that were exactly the same shade.

Sometimes what looks like temperament is merely self-preservation. Many singers, notably Jeritza and the late Caruso, have made a practice of speaking to no one for several hours before singing. The audience benefits here.

An audience, by the way, can raise a performer

245

J a z z

to the seventh heaven or dash him down to hell. I never have faced an intentionally unkind one, but sometimes I have been greatly depressed by coldness and stand-offishness. An audience expects so much. People look at you, not as if you are a human being, but just as if you are something built up for their entertainment. They will never excuse a mistake and they make no allowances for your off-days.

The players don't glare or laugh when the audience applauds in the wrong place, but the audience will laugh at a mistake or even hiss. Perhaps if they understood the handicaps actors and musicians often overcome at a performance they would be more charitable. The other day, I saw a dancer at a vaudeville house fall in a heap in the wings after her turn on the stage. An old sprain had suddenly become painful again while she was doing a difficult whirl at the very beginning of her act, but she kept a smile on her face and went on dancing. She got a few hand claps and, very likely, some former fan of hers turned to his wife and remarked "Well, too bad, that one's getting old and stiff."

A thing I could never understand is how any actor or musician gets the swelled head. God gives talent and those who get it deserve very little credit for it. The applause doesn't last long, either, and then what have we to console our old age with if we are just a mass of conceit?

Do you suppose Al Jolson and Eddie Cantor know how they got to be comedians? Or George Cohan how he became the favorite personality of the stage? Hard work, you say? Well, partly. Good luck? Maybe, a little. But mostly, it's just God-given talent, something to accept humbly and use the best you can.

A lot of folks wonder what a conductor is for, anyway. I've read pieces written by critics who speculated upon how much better certain orchestras would sound if they weren't handicapped by leaders. Well, it may sound a little immodest to say that an orchestra can't do without a leader, but I do say it. I wish the critics could hear a really leaderless orchestra. Only, of course, such a thing is not possible, for if the conductor were not there, some natural born leader would rise from the ranks to guide the rest to safety.

Jazz

A band is like an army. It must have a commander. A good conductor must be a real musician. He should be able to play at least one instrument well and should understand the intricacies and possibilities of all the others he employs. He must be a judge of men—tactful, democratic, and yet able to make his authority felt. He has to be a good showman and likable. If he isn't shamming, it won't hurt for him to be a little eccentric.

As for the ease of jazz conducting—did you ever stand on a space two and a half by two and a half for just one hour? Try it sometime. There have been plenty of days when I've had to do that almost twelve hours at a stretch without any rest.

Here used to be a typical day of mine: Get up at 9 A.M. snatch a bite of breakfast, get to the office by 10. Attack correspondence, attend to details of my orchestra business (I handle a whole string of orchestras that play in New York and other cities). At 12, a rehearsal or phonograph take. At 2, play at the Palace Theater. At 3, another rehearsal or recording session. At 8:30, play the Palace again and after that play the Palais Royal until 3 A.M. The rest of the time I slept.

And mind you, this didn't include the necessary activities for publicity purposes, the people who come bringing letters of introduction or wanting you to hear them play or asking for aid with some charity. And the benefits—mustn't forget them. I have played as many as fifty-nine of these in twenty-six weeks. And yet a writer who is also one of my best friends said one day that I have a cinch of a job—"just standing before an orchestra and patting my foot indifferently well!"

The radio, especially when it first came in, also added to my labors. I played "The Star-Spangled Banner" the first time the national anthem was ever sent through the air. To do it, I had to race madly from the Palais Royal to the radio station. It was Sunday and at the station a minister was making a speech.

They hadn't the system so well organized then as they have it now and apparently nobody had the nerve to tell him he was running over his time. I began to pace the floor, for I had to be back at the Palais Royal at six. But there was no sign the speaker was ever going to stop.

Finally the announcer, an agreeable young blond chap, took matters into his own hands.

"That's all right, I can fix him," he vowed. "Just let him talk on."

He rushed away, did something intricate to a few connections, cut the poor minister off the air entirely, put the orchestra in front of another microphone and we played. Then we rushed back to the Palais Royal and—picked up the minister, still talking.

I have had lots of interesting adventures in the air. Once I gave my mother a birthday party, I in New York, she in Denver listening in at a radio set I had sent her. Another time, my little son sent aerial birthday greetings to me, and one night, at Station WOR in Newark, we played the latest New York jazz hits at three o'clock in the morning for the Prince of Wales, who was listening in at Brook House, London.

A jazz maker is sure of adventure and usually he likes it. Unless, of course, it crowds in too rapidly when he hasn't had more than two or three hours of sleep the night before!

XIII

One-night Jazz Stands

XIII: One-night Jazz Stands

*A*MERICA is in a state of jazz," sonorously proclaim many religious bodies after serious surveys of the saxophone situation.

I toured our forty-eight states recently and am inclined to agree. Only of course, the religious bodies and I are a little at variance in the matter of definition. They regard the whole topic of jazz as deplorable and I cannot, for many reasons, agree with them. By "state of jazz," I merely mean that the entire United States is whistling, singing, playing, eating, and even working, to jazz. Not to speak of undergoing operations and convalescing to it.

Moreover, the jazz interest in the smallest hamlet and biggest city alike is distributed in all directions, so that at concerts, one gets bookworms, bank presidents, village loafers and what not.

A great deal of the interest is only curiosity.

253

J a z z

Much of it never develops into actual enthusiasm and a lot of it is just plain scorn. But at least we are getting people to think about us and argue about us, which is a good sign for any enterprise.

I was more or less dubious when I prepared for a jazz concert tour of the United States. And not the least of my worries was the misgiving with which my twenty-five boys contemplated the trip. Two or three of the new ones had never in their lives been farther from Broadway than Boyle's Thirty Acres in Jersey City, where Jack Dempsey licked Carpentier, and to hear them tell it, they cherished no ambition to better their travel record.

They had, in short, all the real New Yorker's prejudice against "the sticks." Many of my friends shared the feeling. Some who have done time on the two-a-day vaudeville circuits described country hotels. Others, more sympathetic, encouraged me by figuring that I could snatch an occasional respite on Broadway, if life in the provinces grew too difficult. The most confirmed New Yorkers are those who have lived in Manhattan about six months. These boys nearly wore me out with their solicitude. Altogether, I got so many condolences that I began to feel very sorry for myself.

Besides, Paul Whiteman, Jr., had just reached a most interesting age where he could sit up and take notice of me whenever I hove into view. It was about this time that I observed he even seemed to cry for me.

So I felt sort of martyr-like when we set off for our first stop somewhere in Maryland. I think it was in Cumberland that I first had Maryland fried chicken. Either there or Baltimore. Anyway, after that, life looked different.

I could do a whole book on rare foods that my doctor forcibly kept me from devouring as we went along. Chicken and cream gravy at the Claypool Hotel, Indianapolis, hot cakes, doughnuts and strawberry short cake in Denver (mother-made!), wiener wurst and sauerkraut in Minneapolis, cornbread in Louisville—there is no end to the food lore I picked up. But my doctor had a way of condemning all indigenous food as fattening and a rabid prejudice against my getting any fatter. So that mostly, my life between concerts consisted in glimpsing gorgeous food and being forbidden to eat it.

The country we live in makes an interesting movie taken in one-night stands. To my surprise, after all the high-brow fun I'd heard poked at them, Rotary and Kiwanis clubs weren't too awfully bad and I heard lots of pleasant things their members were doing for other people. Nor were these our only cheerful findings about human nature. Hotel men told me that only about one per cent. of the traveling public beats its board bill. A Topeka judge confided that only one man in a hundred beats his wife nowadays. And we hit one town where the citizens swear there isn't a single reformer. No, I won't tell its name. The inhabitants made me promise not to. They don't want any increase in population. Which is another way they are unique.

It's amazing how important a large population is in the American scheme of things. Especially to chambers of commerce. Of course we noticed the chambers of commerce. It is impossible to travel long in the United States without doing that. I never heard so many statistics in my life as I heard from them. I don't suppose anybody ever checks them up, for they say the census takers are very careless and leave out a good part of the population in making a count. I mean the chambers of commerce say this—say it with startling unanimity wherever you go.

I never knew there were so many firsts in the world as there are in this country. Nothing is too small to be first in. For a while I kept the pamphlets and statistics that were lavished upon me about our leading industries, but it seemed, on the whole, that I might eventually have to get an extra baggage car for the instruments if I kept on, so I reluctantly sacrificed the statistics somewhere between San Francisco and St. Paul.

I found out some things that maybe you don't know. Of course, everybody knows that Grand Rapids leads in furniture. But do you realize that it also is first in fly-paper?

I wanted to see the fly-paper factories, but the owner of them was evidently a suspicious person. He wouldn't let me in. I tried to explain that I had no desire to steal his secrets, but they told me that manufacturing fly-paper is a very serious business, with formulæ for stickiness that must be guarded in a vault. Did you ever smell a fly-paper factory? We drove past this one. Terrible!

Battle Creek is another interesting place in Michigan. It leads in doctors and health foods. After dining at one "san" on a substitute for meat, a substitute for sugar, meltoze, sterilized butter and hot malted nuts topped off with minute brew, which is a substitute for a much more exciting drink, I felt so invigorated that I went out and bought an ice cream soda and that led me to discover another thing that Battle Creek is noted for —stands where you can buy ice cream sodas. I fancy it is a reaction from the sanitary atmosphere.

Cities are like people—hard-boiled or timid, down at the heels or neatly mended up, showy or plain, cheerful or glum. Most American cities are cheerful, a little on the boastful side, fairly neat— rather like an American schoolboy who hasn't had many lickings and is a bit over-confident about himself, yet diffident, too, underneath.

In spite of the prosperity, there is no subject so prevalent as a conversation lead everywhere in the United States as "hard times." We spend a deal of energy worrying about trade conditions and the taxes and the younger generation and the Reds and jazz. A good many of us go abroad nowadays—to Paris and London, anyway. That is a sign of the new prosperity. We call it "jumping across the Big Pond," and we are always surprised at ourselves for having the courage to make a trip that once was regarded as entirely the prerogative of the very rich.

I used to make a game of judging from the smoking room conversation what section of the country we were passing through. You could do it, too. Not from the accent so much as from the actual gist of the talk. If he didn't talk at all, you knew he was an Easterner. And in the parts where we were most of the time, he was in the minority. Traveling through the West and Middle West, everybody talked. As you go West, talk is put on and coats and collars are put off. In the Missouri-Kansas-Nebraska sector, you are treated to intimacies from total strangers—and you like it. A Bostonian wouldn't, maybe. But why not? There's a certain benevolence about people who

259

take you into their hearts and tell you their troubles
and their family history.

There were other invariables such as marbled
lobbies. This is something no hotel can be without.
Also there are conventions—another hotel adjunct.
Men standing about uncertainly, wearing badges
and a subdued air—red and white and blue badges.
Earnest talk, vigorous back slaps, self-conscious
guffaws when the talk grows lower in a group.

The American business man is curiously restless
on a holiday. He would rather be home, or at least
back at the office. He keeps long-distancing his
stenographer to be sure everything is going all right
in his absence.

"H'lo, thatchu, Miss Williams? Yah. Say
how's everything going? That so? Well, did
Jones come in? He never? That's funny. That's
awful funny. D'yu call him up? Well, you'd
better, if he don't come in first thing to-morrow.
Huh? Why, certainly it's important, Miss Williams. I got to know what he proposes to do.
No, I won't bother about that. Huh? Well, I tell
you, call Jones up first thing in the morning and
then let me know what he says. And—hello, hello,

Miss Williams, I guess I'll be home a day sooner than I expected. There're several things I'm kinda worried about. Yah—well, don't forget to call Jones. Goo'bye."

Women enjoy a hotel more than men. They like to be free of responsibility and yet be able to summon well-trained servants by pressing a button. Bellboys say women are tipping better—all but the very prettiest ones. These seem to think their beauty is enough.

My favorite hobby on the road was collecting hotel signs. Out in Arizona, I got one that said in large black letters: "Women, do not take men to your rooms. Ladies will not."

In Texas, mine host welcomed us hospitably: "We want you to feel at home. If you spit on the floor at home, spit on the floor here."

It is Illinois where they have some kind of law about all the berths being extra-long. A newspaper man in Springfield suggested that Lincoln, whose home it was, might have been responsible for the law, he being a long man. If he was, that is simply one more benefaction of his to the human race. I got a permanent crick in my back from much scrooging down to fit inadequate beds and sheets.

In New Jersey, we ran across the father of one of the most successful Broadway stars acting as taxi starter in a hotel. In Kansas City, a girl threatened to commit suicide unless we gave her a letter of introduction to David Belasco.

Everywhere we were besieged by youngsters trying to get into jazz bands. Sometimes it was a colored bellboy who proudly informed us that he was running a jazz band on the side. Not infrequently, an ambitious parent of the town's smartest set would bring her boy to play for us. Folks lugged in musical compositions to be judged and instruments to be tuned and tested. We tried to see everybody, because you never know when you will miss a genius.

In Cleveland, we went on trial ourselves—trial by jury. Twelve prominent men and women interested in music, but not professionally connected with it, put us on the witness stand and found us "not guilty of being an absolute menace, but at the same time greatly in need of correction and refinement." Perhaps that was letting us off easy.

JAZZ WITHIN THE LAW

One-night Jazz Stands

It was also in Cleveland that the pupils in the continuation schools handed in written opinions of jazz. A college sophomore said jazz is worth while because it dulls care. And a meat packer taking a course in science said it was all wrong because it dulls the soul.

One of the high spots of the tour for me came in Providence when Rachmaninoff, the Russian composer, postponed a trip for six days to come to our concert. And he liked us, too, so he said.

In Washington, I found out that men are the true supporters of jazz. Miss Jessie MacBride, critic on the Washington *Times*, pointed out that in an afternoon audience more than fifty per cent. were men. That was a record for that city. And later, we found that three-fifths of our Boston audiences were men—middle-aged, too. I thought that was a good argument for jazz. Men don't usually care for concerts.

Boston was one of the surprises the trip held. We were prepared to be frozen out, having heard of the traditional Boston antipathy to innovations. Instead, we had capacity audiences and a request to play an extra performance.

J a z z

One of the oddest concerts was at Williamsport, Pa., where we had a concert scheduled for Sunday evening. Unluckily, the ministers selected us for an issue and hauled out the blue laws which made us illegal on the Sabbath. Then our advance representative, Estella Karn, had an idea. Why not start the concert at a minute past midnight, which would make it Monday morning? We did, with great hilarity and a packed house.

It is hard to tell why an orchestra gives a better performance one time than another. Partly, I suppose, it is the way the members are feeling but mainly, I think, it has to do with the spirit of the audience. And I doubt if we ever played better even in San Francisco or Denver, both of which were home, than we did on our first visit to Chicago. That warm glow that can cross the footlights started out front and ran right back stage. Since then, I've thought of Chicago as the jolly, friendly, self-made millionaire of cities, with the heartiest hand clasp of all.

The Denver concert was the hardest for me. No wonder, for while it's great to get home, there are too many people who know you. You have to be on your toes every minute to make them think you are any good and if you seem to esteem yourself too highly, they're likely to decide you have the bighead.

In Denver, the fellows knew me when I had a paper route and was the champion hotcake and chili eater of the town. Anyway, I showed 'em I could still hold down that record! That show was probably better than the concert, but the concert went off all right, too, except that my voice gave out on me when I tried to make a speech.

New Orleans, being the home of jazz, is interesting to jazzists. There are as many theories about the original jazz band in New Orleans as there are bands in the city to-day. And that is legion.

The most entertaining jazz figure is Stale Bread, a blind jazz musician, who may have invented jazz, for all I know. Stale Bread has a real name —Lacoume, I believe, but nobody ever remembers it. He lost his sight twenty-five years ago and in his blindness has taught himself to play the banjo, the piano, the trap drums, the guitar, the mandolin and the bass viol. His first love is New Orleans, his next, jazz.

"New Orleans is the jazz university of the country," he boasts. "You let a musician tell any bunch in the world that he learned his jazz in New Orleans and they'll give him a chance to show his stuff."

There were eight members of Stale Bread's original band. These were known about town as Piggy, Family Haircut, Warm Gravy, Booze Bottle, Seven Colors, Whiskey and Monk.

The band hang-out was the old Newsboys' Home on Barronne Street. Stale Bread was the organizer. His instruments were a cheese box for a banjo, a soap box guitar, a cigar box violin and a half barrel bass fiddle. He had also an old tambourine, a zither and a harmonica.

The leader trained his gang until the noise they made was adequate even to their small-boy ears. Then he took them out to play on the street. In no time at all, he was blocking traffic. A sour-face complained and a cop pinched the band. He brought them into court and the judge, trying not to laugh, ordered them to play in their own defense.

It was a great moment in the life of the little blind boy. He rose gravely, bowed to "Hizzoner," and the spectators, raised a piece of wood that he used for a baton, and the dirty, ragged eight began. Stale Bread thinks that was the first time any court in the world ever heard jazz. The judge listened solemnly. When the last fearful note died, he turned to the leader.

"Stale Bread," said he, "you may be a band, but you're a spasm band. Discharged."

The name stuck and the spasm band went on playing. Stale Bread is still playing—playing and talking jazz.

John Robichaux and John Piron, New Orleans orchestra leaders who claim to have been present at the birth of jazz, believe that the great American noise started along the water front among natural Negro musicians and developed into the heart and soul of New Orleans.

They are very proud of jazz in New Orleans but critical of visiting brands. "Takes N'Awleens to show 'em real jazz," they maintain.

When we got to St. Louis, we found all the policemen out with guns. For awhile we felt a little uncertain whether this was a greeting or a precaution. It turned out to be merely police drill.

In this Missouri city lives John Stark, original rag man, now eighty-four years old. Mr. Stark still publishes and sells ragtime. He is a gentle soul about everything else, but jazz is anathema to him and jazz makers not much better. He calls his establishment the "classic rag house," and from it, he issued the original "Maple Leaf Rag" of Scott Joplin, purchased for something like fifteen dollars.

We couldn't get Mr. Stark to come to our concert. I have a feeling he may have wished the police had used their guns that day we arrived.

Perhaps, all along the line there were people who shared this sentiment. But I trust and believe not in Texas. In Texas, everybody loves jazz and jazz makers. The hotter the jazz is, the better they like it, too. The only time they resented us was when they got the idea we were trying to be highbrow. We played before Governor Ma Ferguson in Austin. I like women governors—seems to me women are cut out for that sort of thing.

Two of the band were arrested in Texas because

they left their hotel after midnight to get something to eat. They weren't familiar with customs in these wide open spaces.

There are several kinds of risks when you travel with a gang as full of pep as mine. A successful concert demands every player in his place and feeling right up to the mark. So we had to keep out of fights, jails and epidemics. Our doctor usually had the fellows drink ginger ale instead of water, so they wouldn't catch germs. That doctor spent most of his time on my trail, though. He made me cut out meat, bread and potatoes. If I was very good, he let me have a second helping of spinach every other day. Once I lost fifty pounds and got down to 230.

I think our tour was one of the longest ever attempted by a full orchestra. We played every town and city of any note in the North and South all the way through El Paso to Los Angeles and San Francisco and then back through the Middle West. In Jackson, Mississippi, Billy Sunday closed church to come out and hear us.

Lots of courtesies were shown us and we had a good time, though we worked hard. The "family" got to be great little jokers and we used always to be playing silly pranks on one another with the audience sometimes in on the joke, sometimes not.

One evening I put some black gum on my front teeth, making it look as if three or four were out, and the boys nearly broke down from laughter. The next night, while I was off stage, they rigged themselves out in whiskers made of false hair as an impromptu surprise for me.

The tour turned me into a perpetual information bureau. Girls wanted to know what was the Prince of Wales' favorite musical instrument and were his eyes really blue?

"Will saxophone playing injure the voice?" anxious mothers asked. "How do you organize a jazz band?" "Do you really make as much money as the paper said?" "Can you recommend a hotel in New York where I could go with two children? I have heard lots of hotels in New York don't allow children."

I got used to speaking to women's clubs and shaving in a rocking Pullman, though I was heckled sometimes by the clubs and cut myself a time or two at the shaving.

One-night Jazz Stands

I wouldn't take anything for my months on the road. I feel that I know America and Americans better than I ever did before. I believe I can conduct an orchestra better because of my one-night standing and I am going to do it over every year until I've proved that jazz is music.

XIV

The Future of Jazz

XIV: The Future of Jazz

$\mathcal{W}$HAT will be the end of jazz? I don't
know. Nobody knows. One may only
speculate. Perhaps my ideas on such a nebulous
subject are as likely to be sound as the next man's.
I don't know.

Anyway, I am no prophet. I can only say what
seems to me possible and a very little probable.

First of all, jazz has a chance because it is a
sheer Americanism. Artistic Europe grants this
and applauds. Have Europeans ever accepted any
other music of ours? Alas, no! We have assim-
ilated the arts of Europe, yet made none of them
our own. As W. J. Henderson, New York musical
critic, puts it: "Up to the beginning of the nineteenth century, we produced nothing which still
moves before us."

If we made a play, it was patterned after Far-
quhar, or Sheridan. When we painted a portrait,

275

we fixed a reverent gaze on Sir Joshua Reynolds. When we fashioned a public building, we bowed before the shrines of Wren and Gibbs.

Our music followed the same lines. And that is not the best way. We'd not have had a Ford if we had been satisfied with European ways—nor perhaps a phonograph, nor a steamboat, nor a sky-scraper. It is something to branch out at last for ourselves in music as in other efforts. This does not mean of course that we shall immediately create art. But then, neither does the fact that many look upon jazz as a sort of artistic blasphemy mean that it is so. We jazzists might reply to those who are shocked at what they call bizarre sounds evoked by our instruments, as Turner did to his lady critic.

"Mr. Turner," said the dame, "I never see such colors in the sunset as you see."

"Don't you wish you could, ma'am?" reparteed the painter.

Turner was ahead of his generation and knew it. Perhaps we jazzists are ahead of ours. But I must confess in all humbleness that we have moments when we doubt this as much as any of those who cavil.

We are encouraged occasionally by musicians like Leopold Stokowski, John Alden Carpenter and Fritz Kreisler who tell us that jazz will live. We wish there were more of them writing jazz. They could answer the jeers directed at our infant art better by composition than by words.

Not that I for one am greatly affected by criticism. Was it not Mendelssohn who, when asked what was the root of the strong discord at the opening of the "Wedding March," replied, "I don't know and I don't care." Even the law-abiding Haydn called the rules of music his servants and wrote consecutive fifths that must have shocked the academic of the time.

When Beethoven began his first symphony with a discord, all the orthodox were scandalized. They might even have accused him of "jazzing it up," if the phrase had been invented then. The new is always bearing the brunt of our human tendency to find fault. That doesn't matter. What does matter is that there have been advances in jazz which prove that the material has something worth while. The soft jazz rhythms of the present day represent great progress from the crudities of ten years ago.

Because it must be played by Americans to be well-played, jazz is giving the young musician his chance. It will continue to do that. It has already compelled the musical world to take George Gershwin seriously. He has been commissioned to write for the New York Symphony. But he was never taken seriously until the "Rhapsody in Blue," though he had been writing musical revues and popular songs for a long time.

Some day, it will be with jazz here as it is with the races in England. Everybody who can scrape together a few shillings goes to the races. They are a national institution. Jazz will be an American national institution.

Every boy, whether he is normally musically inclined or not, wants to learn to play something. Jazz has given him the opportunity of his life and something is going to come of it. Perhaps that something will be a new art. Certainly it will be a good deal of musical composition, some of it very bad and some of it, I hope, very good.

Teaching the Young How to Jazz

The Future of Jazz

Will it be possible eventually to establish chairs of jazz in universities? I do not see why not. My conception of a college is a place which teaches its students that which will be useful and pleasant for them to know. Jazz music is certainly useful. Players who have worked their way through college blowing a saxophone or twanging a banjo can often step into jobs that pay $75 or $100 a week. I mean jazz banding jobs. Tell me any other occupation that starts the June graduate off at any such salary.

An example of the financial possibilities of the jazz band is furnished by Roger Wolfe Kahn, son of Otto Kahn, wealthy New York banker and art patron. This youth of seventeen has an income of $1,000 a week from his five bands, while his friends, starting in to learn the banking business from the bottom up, receive less than a quarter of his weekly wage per month.

One of the first concerts my orchestra played after the début at Aeolian Hall was a benefit for the Academy at Rome. The story got about that the money taken in was to be used to establish a chair of jazz at the foreign institution. A lot of people got terribly excited. They wrote letters to the newspapers and inveighed against such a scheme, predicting the fall of everything that was high and holy in music. I hope they will live to see what a jazz chair will do to civilization. For I think they may be agreeably surprised.

One thing must happen before the future of jazz can be assured. That is, the critics must stop comparing jazz and symphony orchestras. Such a comparison is not fair. The symphony is one thing in instrumentation, scoring and direction. We are quite another. To my mind comparing us is almost as silly as the talk of a jazz opera. I do not believe there can be a real jazz opera. There is too much contradiction of terms. The very theme of jazz is unfitted to opera. The operatic form was built for folk lore. You can't fit such a form to the romance, say, of the skyscraper which is, after all, an expression of jazz.

Nor do I see why anybody would want to. Every honest musician must concede that grand opera is the worst possible form of music. In fact, it is not music at all—it is a hash of music, drama and tableau in which they all are debased. Think of gargling for half an hour to express the simple fact that one is hungry. Yet that, or an equal absurdity, is what happens in every known opera. Opera is one of my favorite sports when I have time to spend at it, but nobody can deny that its music moves slowly, held back and forced to mark time while the drama catches up with it and the stage hands shift scenery. Jazz does not move slowly. Anything written around a jazz theme would have to be a musical show, not an opera. I do not see why we should not have this. But for goodness' sake, let's throw away the old forms and create our own new ones.

Either jazz is something that can dispense with known forms and make a form of its own, or else it is nothing. America has a marvelous chance just now to get even with Europe. For the first time, Europeans are interested in something besides our dollar. They eat up our simplest jazz trick. When I was in France a few years ago, the Paris Conservatory sent a representative to ask for jazz scores for their library. I suggested other American compositions to them, but they said they wanted jazz.

All the records of the past seem, if not to point

to the future greatness of jazz, at least to argue that it has a chance. When Wagner's music was first presented, it was even more revolting to the esthetic ear than jazz is now. Clara Schumann in 1879 confided to her diary: "I have been glancing through a number of new musical productions and feel depressed. The influence of Wagner is far-reaching and injurious. No one cares any more for melody. The way people fling harmony about is something terrible. Resolutions are considered unnecessary."

And then there was the sarabande. To-day the word brings up to most of our minds the slow and stately rhythms of Bach or Händel. It makes us think of noble and dignified strains in sonatas and operas of the eighteenth century. Yet the sarabande, when the restless younger generation in the Spain of 1588 took to dancing it, was more of a blow to the orthodox than is the most shocking jazz to-day to the same class.

Father Mariana, writing in 1609, accused the sarabande of having done more harm than the bubonic plague which devastated Europe in the Middle Ages. Yet eventually this outrageous affront to the morals of the unco' guid became the inspiration for some of the greatest musical composers.

The Waltz had almost as stormy an introduction. Lord Byron had something to say of this innovation:

"Not soft Herodias, with winding tread, her nimble feet
    danced off another's head;
Not Cleopatra on her galley's deck, displayed so much of
    limb or more of neck
Than thou, ambrosial waltz."

Perhaps these instances of the past prove nothing, after all, except the need for a certain generosity and tolerance. Still, if one were attempting to be a prophet, it might not be bad logic to predict that some day jazz will mean what sarabande does to-day. At any rate, jazz, though maligned, is in a better position than were the German operas in France during the period that a man could be put into jail for whistling one of them.

There is a parallel of the past to be drawn, too, between jazz and folk songs. What folk song would have amounted to anything if some great writer had not put it into a symphony? Jazz wears elaborate garments well, too. Why may one not hope to see it one day dressed in the best? Not in symphony, but in some new and equally beautiful garment of its own. Folk songs are simple melodies. The harmonic setting is wholly unimportant, yet these tunes have been used as themes by the greatest. Jazz is elemental, too. Like the folk song, it meets and satisfies an undeveloped esthetic and emotional craving.

A further comfort for those who hope for something better in the future of jazz lies in the fact that the jazz music movement is accompanied by the same tendency in art and literature. A movement so widespread seems bound by all the laws of chance to contribute something of permanence.

Sometimes I am asked how the jazzists will average when the pendulum swings back as many think it will and the standard becomes "thought rather than spirits, quality rather than color, knowledge rather than irreticence, intelligence rather than singularity, wit rather than romp, precision rather than surprise, and dignity rather than impudence."

I confess I do not see why these should be the standards. After all emotion is the foundation of

art as it is of life. And certainly jazz has enough
of emotion and to spare.

I wish our jazz discussions could spare the in-
vectives. Even defending jazz, one is inclined to
be defiant. If one could remain amused and aloof,
it would accomplish more—letting, as a Washington reviewer put it, "the nose glasses fight over
whether or not jazz is music."

"One can take it or leave it," adds this irreverent
critic, "for here it is, thumbing its snippy nose at
the sticks-in-the-mud, the high and holy. If it is
just a glorious joke on elderly musicians, it is a
good one."

I like to remember that it was after he had heard
my orchestra that Dr. Leopold Stokowski, inter-
nationally known conductor of the Philadelphia
symphony, gave out an interview declaring that
jazz had come to stay. He did not prophesy that
jazz itself would ascend to true greatness, but held
that it was an epoch-making influence, the tendency
of which might bring about a revolution in the
whole world of music. He predicted that, through
the influence of America, the entire art will be vul-
garized in the best sense of the word and enter

more and more into the daily life of the people, influencing them and becoming part of their philosophy. He pointed out three obvious trends which have sprung from jazz.

First, he said, there is a movement toward the quarter tone which will either necessitate the rebuilding of all instruments now in use or a reform in the method of their use since to play it requires an instrument for many hands.

The second trend was toward the development of color in music with the eventual combination of visual color symphonies and tonal effects.

Third, he saw the development of music into multiple forms in which there would be the elimination of prohibition in music so that all forms would be permitted, with the result of greater variety to appeal to all sorts of people.

The quarter tone idea in music is of particular interest to the orchestra. The orchestra is obviously the one and only "musical instrument with many hands." May not jazz development therefore lend a widespread movement toward community play? Instead of one musician with piano and violin, two, three, four or six persons may play together, indeed must play together if they are to use the greatly extended, beautifully flexible scale of greater tones. Thus, perhaps music will be put back into its proper place in the home and the community, making it in American towns what it is already in European village life—a vital factor. Perhaps that is far-fetched but it seems to me it might come.

I am ambitious for jazz to develop always in an American way. I want to see compositions written around the great natural and geographical features of American life—written in the jazz idiom. I believe this would help Americans to appreciate their own country—their Hudson, their Grand Canyon, their Painted Desert. There is thematic material in each of these. True, we have no lorelized rocks, no mouse castles on the Hudson. That is because we are not old enough. We must make traditions. It is time we began. Jazz can help by catching our national themes fast in composition.

I want jazz to give the young musician his chance. The unknown composer has to pay to get his compositions played by a good symphony. And he usually has no money—so his chance is gone. I hope jazz is going to give him his chance. It must for its hope lies in him—in youth.

The charge that has been made is true—jazz is all dressed up and has hardly any place to go. That is because so few composers are writing for it. The best of them are too old and serious-minded for jazz. They don't dance. They don't catch the rhythm of the younger generation. We must look to the young folks for the jazz compositions of the future. We must see that music becomes as much an education staple in this country as reading or spelling. Who goes to symphony concerts to-day? Except for music students, mostly men and women over forty.

There is only one way to educate an American except in his chosen line. That way is by entertainment. And we must start the entertainment in the school room. Since the high-brow composer will not write jazz music, we must train the popular composer to become a better musician. We must teach the rhythmic invention, the contrapuntal construction and formal variety needed in the best of jazz composition. When this is done, I venture to say that the future of modern American music will reveal itself soon enough.

Of course, what jazz really needs is a fairy god-mother to endow it. So far there has been no chance to take time off for experimentation. No millionaire has come forward to offer the necessary funds for laboratory work. It is not so easy to keep only the best when one must at the same time be thinking of how to make one's bread and butter. But we shall keep trying—until perhaps we find the fairy godmother!

XV

As for Me

XV: As for Me

*A*RE you really going to devote your life to jazz?" asked a friend who hates jazz.

I didn't answer at once because I never before had looked so far ahead—but when the answer did come, it was yes.

I don't know exactly what my life will be worth to jazz, but such as it is, I offer it gladly. Jazz has been good to me. As they say in the cigarette ads, it satisfies. It gives me, first, a medium of musical expression. It affords a field for experimentation. It has won me a certain amount of recognition among people whose opinion I esteem and it has paid me well financially. In this last respect, it is a good deal more profitable to lead a jazz orchestra than to be president.

And when I see what a worry it is to be president, I can't help preferring my own job. On the whole, I have rather a full and interesting life as

293

does any man who is doing work he likes. I live in the country in summer, near enough the ocean so that I can get a swim after work. I am a dub at golf, but possess one friend I can beat.

I find time occasionally for the theater, books (mostly on music), romps with my boy, talks with my wife—just a commonplace American man. If it were not too trite, I should say here that my wife is my best pal and severest critic. Mrs. Whiteman was, before her marriage, Vanda Hoff, a well-known dancer, and she knows and loves music. She goes to all our rehearsals and tells me how terrible they are.

I get mad, of course, and she calmly keeps on talking. In spite of myself, I listen and generally end by thinking pretty much as she does. The only time we really quarrel is when she threatens to throw out my locomotives which she says mess up the house.

I shall go blithely on insisting that jazz is the real American music. To prove my assertion, I shall play all of it that I can lay my hands on, the more pretentious the better. Young composers may have the assurance at all times that ours is one organization from which the native product may get a hearing. Whether jazz will make music or not cannot be settled by arguing about it. The only way is to try it out.

I have dozens of experiments to make with jazz. I am convinced that it has therapeutic value. I believe a way will be found to use it in curing diseases of mind and body, especially melancholia that amounts eventually to insanity. Music has been used by Southern planters of all time to speed up work among the negroes—used to such an extent that special song leaders were hired on the same basis as workmen.

So far there has been no serious attempt to employ music in practical everyday life. I think this will all come. Already it has been ascertained that a person totally deaf gets certain vibrations from jazz music which raise the pulse beat and produce all the symptoms of exhilaration.

Being a jazz missionary is not the easiest job in life. Frankly, the ultimate purpose is to raise the public taste until it will accept a full evening of serious music. But it is a ticklish business, trying to put jazz in the position of being recognized as a serious medium.

On the one hand, we must not dash at once into music that sends away the very ones we want to educate. On the other, we must not offend the persons whose approval we need. So for a time, our progress must be a compromise.

Meantime, there is considerable cheering news from the front. Siegfried Wagner, son of the famous writer of music drama, who visited this country not so very long ago, thinks jazz "is a step to real musical achievement." Levitski, well-know pianist, plays jazz for his own amusement, and Mrs. Kreisler complains that since her husband discovered jazz, he scarcely ever practices—just plays jazz. Eva Gauthier, singer, has placed jazz on her concert programs. Darius Milhaud and Igor Stravinski have been influenced by jazz rhythms in their work and admit it. We have Leo Sowerby, young American composer, doing "Synconata" and other pieces for the jazz orchestra, and and Ernest Schelling, John Alden Carpenter, Cole Porter, Deems Taylor, George Gershwin and Ferde Grofe experimenting with the idiom.

Once in a while, too, comes a letter like the one from Rudolph Gans, conveying kindly sentiments about what we are trying to do and adding: "I can listen to well-written and well-played jazz for quite a while with pleasure, sometimes with emotion."

To be sure, Mr. Gans presently admits, "and then I get tired of it, to say the least. But so would I feel overcome by a program of purely sentimental romantic music. Anyway, legitimate dance music has never been so beautifully symphonic as now and has never been as melodically and harmonically satisfying as in the outstanding works written in jazz form and jazz spirit to-day. Melodically, however, it has been to a great extent at the expense of the recognized masters of music. This is to be regretted."

For the rest, there is at least one place in the world where tired ears may rest assured they will not hear jazz strains. That is in an English jail. I hear that the Commissioners of Prisons for Great Britain have banned all jazz music, finding it too amusing.

However, I shall not try a British jail as a jazz

refuge. When I am finished with jazz, or it is finished with me, I shall retire to a certain ranch near
Denver—a ranch that jazz built—and there, perhaps—who knows?—spend my declining years
among the classics.

THE END

POPULAR CULTURE IN AMERICA

1800-1925

An Arno Press Collection

Alger, Jr., Horatio. **Making His Way; Or Frank Courtney's Struggle Upward.** n. d.

Bellew, Frank. **The Art of Amusing:** Being a Collection of Graceful Arts, Merry Games, Odd Tricks, Curious Puzzles, and New Charades. 1866

Browne, W[illiam] Hardcastle. **Witty Sayings By Witty People.** 1878

Buel, J[ames] W[illiam]. **The Magic City:** A Massive Portfolio of Original Photographic Views of the Great World's Fair and Its Treasures of Art . . . 1894

Buntline, Ned [E. Z. C. Judson]. **Buffalo Bill; And His Adventures in the West.** 1886

Camp, Walter. **American Football.** 1891

Captivity Tales. 1974

Carter, Nicholas [John R. Coryell]. **The Stolen Pay Train.** n. d.

Cheever, George B. **The American Common-Place Book of Poetry,** With Occasional Notes. 1831

Sketches and Eccentricities of Colonel David Crockett, of West Tennessee. 1833

Evans, [Wilson], Augusta J[ane]. **St. Elmo: A Novel.** 1867

Finley, Martha. **Elsie Dinsmore.** 1896

Fitzhugh, Percy Keese. **Roy Blakeley On the Mohawk Trail.**
1925

Forester, Frank [Henry William Herbert]. **The Complete Manual For Young Sportsmen.** 1866

Frost, John. **The American Speaker:** Containing Numerous Rules, Observations, and Exercises, on Pronunciation, Pauses, Inflections, Accent and Emphasis . . . 1845

Gauvreau, Emile. **My Last Million Readers.** 1941

Haldeman-Julius, E[manuel].**The First Hundred Million.**
1928

Johnson, Helen Kendrick. **Our Familiar Songs and Those Who Made Them.** 1909

Little Blue Books. 1974

McAlpine, Frank. **Popular Poetic Pearls,** and Biographies of Poets. 1885

McGraw, John J. **My Thirty Years in Baseball.** 1923

Old Sleuth [Harlan Halsey]. **Flyaway Ned; Or, The Old** Detective's Pupil. A Narrative of Singular Detective Adventures.
1895

Pinkerton, William A[llan]. **Train Robberies, Train Robbers, and the "Holdup" Men.** 1907

Ridpath, John Clark. **History of the United States,** Prepared Especially for Schools. Grammar School Edition, 1876

The Tribune Almanac and Political Register for 1876. 1876

Webster, Noah. **An American Selection of Lessons in Reading and Speaking.** Fifth Edition, 1789

Whiteman, Paul and Mary Margaret McBride. **Jazz.** 1926